Dictionary of
Architecture

BROCKHAMPTON PRESS
LONDON

This edition published 1995 by Brockhampton Press, a member of
the Hodder Headline PLC Group.

ISBN 1 86019 004 9

Printed and bound in Slovenia.

A

abacus a flat stone slab forming the uppermost part of a CAPITAL, which may be shaped or moulded in different ways according to the order in which it belongs.

the abacus of a Corinthian capital

abbey a type of monastery, a Christian order comprising a community of monks or nuns presided over by an Abbot or Abbess. The term describes the buildings themselves and also the way of life and purposes of its members. The monastic way of life reached its height in Britain during the early 14th century with many religious communities governed by different Orders, being established at this time. The most familiar of these Orders include the Cistercian, Benedictine, Carthisian, Augustinian, Friars, Knights of St. John and Premonstratensian. After the dissolution of the monasteries, many of the churches and buildings were allowed to decay, especially those in more isolated country areas. However, during the last 150 years repair work to halt the process of decline has been carried out and many fine examples still exist such as Fountains Abbey (Yorkshire), Glastonbury Abbey (Somerset), Dryburgh Abbey (Berwickshire) and Tintern Abbey (Gwent). Some abbey churches in more populated areas fared better and were retained as churches or cathedrals, e.g. Westminster Abbey. *See also* MONASTERY.

abutment the mass or solid construction of stone or brickwork from which an ARCH or VAULT arises, and which supports the lateral pressure or thrust which this exerts. It may be solid rock, a wall or pier depending upon the type of construction.

acroteria pedestals or plinths for ornaments such as statues placed on the apex and lower ends of PEDIMENTS. Also, in GOTHIC architecture, they are sometimes found on the GABLES.

an acrotera from the temple of Minerva at Agipa

adit an entrance or approach to a building.

addorsed two similar or identical figures, usually of animals or creatures from mythology, placed exactly back to back. These ornamental figures are often found on CAPITALS and FRIEZES.

adobe bricks made of clay or mud often containing chopped straw, which are dried in the sun but not baked and are commonly used for the walls of buildings in South and Central America. Lima Cathedral in Peru is constructed of adobe, and the term is used to describe the clay itself as well as the finished bricks.

adytum an inner room, chamber or sanctuary in a Greek TEMPLE.

aedicule in terms of pure classical architecture, a shrine or small room. An aedicule later came to describe a niche used as a shrine, flanked on either side by a column on top of which is an ENTABLATURE and PEDIMENT. The shrine contained a statue and was part of a temple. In Renaissance architecture an aedicule is further broadened to describe any similar ornate opening, such as a window or doorway, which is flanked by columns that support overlying structures which are usually moulded or ornamental.

aerated concrete a modern building material composed of fine sand, chemical components and fuel ash which is placed in moulds and auto-claved to produce lightweight blocks. These are easy to cut and work with and have good insulating properties due to their cellular nature.

affronted the opposite situation to ADDORSED describing two similar or identical figures, usually of animals or creatures from mythology but which are placed so that they exactly face one another. These ornamental figures are often found on CAPITALS and FRIEZES.

aisle it is derived from the Latin word *ala* meaning wing which is a shortened form of *axilla*. In medieval times, *axilla* became *ascella* and was used to described a corridor or wing of a building. Later, the word became associated with a division at the side of a church, runnning along the length of the building and divided off by an ARCADE or COLONNADE of pillars. Aisles often occur on both sides of the church, alongside the central choir and nave, with a roof at a much lower level than that of the main building.

alabaster a beautiful, fine-grained type of gypsum (limestone) which varies in colour from yellow/white to red/brown and is translucent and may be delicately marked. It is soft and readily worked and, cut very thinly, was used in windows in medieval churches, especially in Italy. It was also used as a fine decorative stone inside churches and great houses, especially for columns and sculptures.

alcove a word derived from the Spanish *alcoba* meaning a recessed chamber, sometimes vaulted, within a bedroom, which itself stems from the Arabic word for vault, *alqobbah*. In English architecture an alcove describes a small, vaulted recess separated from the main part of the room by an entrance or partition. The term is also used to describe a recess in a garden, or a bower, often containing a seat.

almshouse a type of house or, usually, group of houses built by a wealthy benefactor to assist the poor and elderly within his parish. Many almshouses were built in the

1500s and 1600s, most as a memorial to their founder. They eventually replaced the monasteries in the role of givers of charity and alms. The buildings vary from simply a row of small cottages to dwellings built around a central courtyard incorporating a chapel and hall. Some are more elaborate with gables facing the street and a gatehouse. The style and grandeur of an almshouse often reflected the wealth and status of its founder and patron.

altar derived from the Latin word *altare*, meaning a raised, high place, the altar was a structure on which offerings (usually of food or drink) were placed and sacrifices made to a god. In the Greek and Roman cultures, altars were often made of marble or stone and varied in construction. In the time of the Early Christian Church an altar was often constructed over the tomb of a saint. In medieval times it was usually built of stone or marble, rectangular in shape and supposedly containing the remains or relics of a saint. Portable altars constructed of metal were also in use at that time. From the Reformation onwards, communion tables made of wood were commonly used in British churches, replacing the earlier stone altars. In medieval times the altars themselves were often carved and highly decorated and many also had an ornamental screen behind attached to the wall. This screen, known as a *reredos*, was often richly carved or decorated with beautifully painted panels and figures in stone and wood. Some of the finest examples dating from the Baroque period are to be found in churches in Germany, Spain and Austria.

alure a walkway or passage especially that behind the

parapet of a fortified castle wall, or around a church roof.

ambulatory a roofed passage for walking in, generally within a church and used originally on processional occasions. The ambulatory often follows a semicircular or polygonal plan in European churches, surrounding the APSE and running behind the High ALTAR. In British churches the ambulatory is usually square in design.

amphitheatre a type of Roman theatre constructed on a circular or elliptical plan, with an ARENA at the base encircled by tiers of seats rising up above. The early amphitheatres were of wood but these were later replaced by solid constructions in stone. The greatest of the amphitheatres in Rome, popularly called the Colosseum, was able to seat an audience of around 50,000 people. A wall 15 feet high surrounded the arena and beneath it was a hollow space where wild animals, equipment and scenery were kept. The outer walls show the CLASSICAL ORDER of four tiers of columns with the DORIC at ground level, then IONIC followed by CORINTHIAN and, at the top, Corinthian with PILASTER form. The lower three tiers had archways between the columns which originally contained statues. All Roman towns of any size and importance had an amphitheatre in which various kinds of spectacular events were staged including gladiator contests, fights with wild animals and processions and exhibitions. Some are still in use today especially for the performance of opera and for bullfights.

annular a ring-shaped vault or passageway.

antechurch an extension or outer part of the west end of a church or chapel, e.g. in the college chapels of Cambridge and Oxford.

antecourt an outer court before the main court of a great mansion.

antefixae decorative ornamental tiles concealing the ends and edges of roof tiles, situated above the eaves. They were generally composed of terracotta but were also frequently made of marble.

an antefixae from the Propylæum at Athens

anteroom a small room forming an outer chamber to a more important, larger room within a mansion.

anticlastic a surface that curves in opposite ways (convex and concave) and in different directions through any given point, e.g. hyperbolic paraboloid roof.

apex stone also known as the saddle stone, this is the uppermost stone in a gable end.

apophyge the slight concave curve at the end of a column where it joins the ASTRAGEL at the top and the FILLET above the base or CAPITAL at the bottom.

apron a raised panel, situated directly below a window sill, which may be ornamental and shaped and is often a Renaissance feature.

apse a feature of church architecture which is a termination, usually of a chapel or chancel, often having a polygonal or semicircular shape and normally domed or vaulted. It is derived from the BASILICA of ancient Rome, and became an integral part of early Christian churches which were themselves based upon this design. In British churches from the early Gothic period onwards it became more usual for a square termination to be used. *See also* AMBULATORY.

aqueduct a man-made structure, usually a series of high arches made from stone or bricks supporting a channel for carrying water. Aqueducts were invented by the Romans for bringing a water supply into a city, an example being the one at Segovia in Spain.

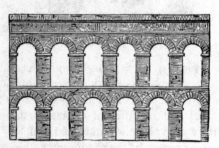

part of a Roman aqueduct

arcade a series of arches supported by COLUMNS, PIERS or PILASTERS which may be a decorative feature against a wall (a blind arcade). An arcade is particularly associated with church architecture and also refers to the division of arches separating the nave from the aisles. Blind arcades may occur on both the exterior and interior walls of churches and may be highly decorated.A covered-over area containing shops, usually featuring a high, vaulted roof and constructed using metal and glass, which became a feature of many cities in the 19th century.

an interlacing blind arcade

arch an opening which is constructed without the use of a lintel. True arches have a curved shape and are constructed out of wedge-shaped blocks which support one another by downward and outward pressure. They are able to support considerable loads. All the wedge-shaped blocks or bricks which form the arch are called the *voussoirs*. The horizontal voussoirs at the base of the arch on either side are called the springers and the central, often larger, one at the top the keystone. The springing line is the level at which the arch rises from its supports.

typical arch support

The supports or solid construction upon which the arch rests are called the ABUTMENTS. A projecting form of moulding on top of the abutments called the impost is often present marking the level of the springing line. The inner curve of the arch, formed by the innermost faces of the voussoirs, is called the *intrados*. The outer curve, formed by the outermost surfaces of the *voussoirs*, is called the *extrados*. The whole of the under surface or roof of the arch is known as the soffit. The distance between the abutments, from one side of the arch to the other, is known as the span. The rise is the greatest height achieved by the arch measured from the springing line to the undersurface of the keystone. There are many different types of arch, some of which are variations of a particular design.

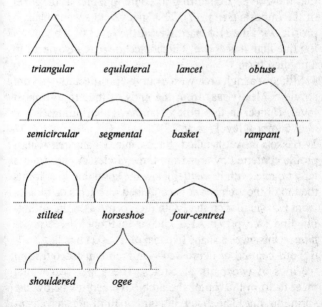

triangular   *equilateral*   *lancet*   *obtuse*

semicircular   *segmental*   *basket*   *rampant*

stilted   *horseshoe*   *four-centred*

shouldered   *ogee*

basic types and styles of arch

1. Semicircular—an arch in the shape of a semicircle with the centre in the middle point of the springing line (*see* p.17).

2. Segmental—an arch in the shape of a segment of a circle which has its centre beneath the springing line. A segmental pointed arch has its profile conferred by the arcs of two circles with centres below the springing line (*see* p.17).

3. Horseshoe—a type of arch especially associated with Islamic buildings and in Spain. It has a circular shape, but the centre of the circle is above the springing line so that the curves are starting to come together at the level of the imposts (*see* p.17). This gives a horseshoe-shaped profile with the arch narrower at the level of the springing line than it is above. The horseshoe may also occur in a pointed form.

4. Stilted—a high arch with a curved profile at the top but straight sides (PIERS) from the ends of the arc to impost level. Hence, in this type of arch, the springing line is above impost level (*see* p.17).

5. Basket, basket-handled, three-centred—an arch with a profile conferred by arcs from three circles. An arc from a larger circle, with its centre below the springing line, forms the top of the arch and it is continued on each side by arcs from two smaller circles, with their centres on the springing line (*see* p.17). Also known in French as *Anse de panier*, this gives a shape like that of a basket handle.

6. Four-centred or depressed—an arch constructed from the arcs of two pairs of circles. The upper two which meet to form the top of the arch have centres below the springing line. The lower and outer pair of arcs have centres on the springing line.

7. Equilateral or pointed—an arch with a profile conferred by the arcs of a pair of identical large circles meeting at the top to form a point. The centre of each circle is at the impost level on the opposite side. The radius of each is the same as the span of the arch (*see* p.17).

8. Obtuse or drop—similar to the equilateral, with a profile conferred by the arcs of a pair of identical circles which meet at the top to form the point. However, in the obtuse or drop arch, the centres of the circles are each within the arch at an identical distance from the imposts along the springing line on either side. This produces a lowered arch with a span greater than the radii of the circles (*see* p.17).

9. Lancet or Early English—similar to the equilateral, with a profile conferred by the arcs of a pair of large identical circles which meet at the top to form the point. However, in the lancet arch the centres of the circles are outside the arch at an identical distance from the sides along a continuation of the springing line. This produces a raised arch with a span less than the radii of the circles (*see* p.17). It was used extensively in England in the early medieval period e.g. for church windows.

10. Ogee or Keel—a pointed arch with a profile conferred by the arcs of two pairs of circles, each pair running in an opposite way to the other. The upper pair of arcs, which meet to form the point, give a concave profile. The centres of their circles are outside and above the arch, on a level with the point and equidistant from it. The pair of lower arcs give a convex profile to that part of the arch. The centres of their much smaller circles are within the arch, along the springing line, at an equal distance on either side from the imposts. (*see* p.17) This type

of arch was first used in the 1300s and became popular in England in the 1400s. A NODDING OGEE ARCH is one in which the apex of the point is further extended.

11. Shouldered, false or corbel—not a true arch but one with a straight lintel at the top supported on either side by a pair of CORBELS which have been carved out to produce a curved, convex or concave profile. Below the curves, the sides of the opening continue straight down. The corbels connect the lintel with the JAMBS of a doorway (*see* p.17).

12. Rampant or raking—an arch with a profile conferred by the arcs of two non-identical circles which meet to form a point at the top. One impost and springing level is higher than the other to produce an asymmetrical profile (*see* p.17).

13. Recessed or compound—usually a doorway composed of a serious of concentric arches set one behind the other to form a broad opening, the dimensions of which gradually reduce from front to back.

14. Foil—including trefoil, cinquefoil and multifoil, where several arcs of circles are used to produce an ornate effect usually for smaller openings. It is a feature associated in particular with Moorish architecture but also in Britain in Romanesque and Gothic buildings.

15. Triangular or mitre—an arch shaped like a triangle formed by two slabs which slope towards one another and meet in a mitre at the top (*see* p.17). It is a type particularly associated with Saxon architecture.

16. Straight—a rectangular opening with a lintel composed of radiating *voussoirs* in the style of an arch.

17. Rowlock—a type of arch with *voussoirs* in separate concentric rings.

18. Strainer—an arch, usually across an aisle or nave of a church, inserted to stop the walls from leaning.

19. Relieving or discharging—a triangular or round arch built onto the wall above an archway or other opening to relieve excess pressure. It is often of segmental type.

20. Skew—an arch with jambs that are not set at right angles to its faces.

21. Tudor—a type of FOUR-CENTRED ARCH popular in the Tudor period in which the upper pair of arcs are nearly flat.

architrave the lintel running from one PIER or COLUMN to another. Also, the lower of the three main portions of an ENTABLATURE. The term is used, less accurately, to refer to the wooden, moulded frame around a door or window.

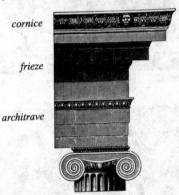

cornice

frieze

architrave

arena correctly, the central circular space of an AMPHITHEATRE but also used to describe any similar structure, such as might be used for sport.

arris a sharp edge produced when two curved or flat surfaces meet as in a V-shaped gutter.

ashlar blocks of building stone, which are worked so that the edges are square and the faces even, that are laid out in horizontal series. Ashlar was first used by the Egyptians in 3 BC.

astragal a type of small, semicircular moulding which marks the division between a column shaft and the capital above. It may be ornamental with bead and reel decoration as in Greek and Roman classical ornament. The term is also applied to the moulding dividing the faces of the architrave of an ENTABLATURE.

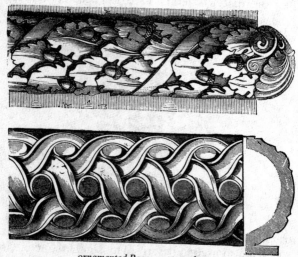

ornamented Roman astragals

astylar a type of classical façade which lacks PILASTERS or COLUMNS.

atrium in the domestic architecture of ancient Roman times, the atrium was an open, inner courtyard surrounded on all sides by the roof. In early church and medieval architecture, the atrium was an entrance court, usually rectangular and flanked by columns. Some modern buildings have a form of atrium in their design.

Plan of a house showing the position of the atrium, marked A (b=bedroom; e=entrance; s=shop)

B

baguette or **bagnette** a small moulding, like an ASTRAGAL, with a semicircular profile. In addition, a frame with small BEAD MOULDING.

bailey *or* **ward** an open court or space within a stone-built castle.

balcony a type of platform extending out from the wall of a building, usually guarded on the free sides by a protective and ornamental BALUSTRADE or railing. It is supported on columns, brackets or may be CANTILEVERED. A very small, ornamental balcony surrounding a window is called a balconette.

a balcony at Cairo

baldachine, baldacchino or **baldaquin** a canopy above an altar, throne or doorway which is suspended from the ceiling or projects from a wall and is supported on columns, brackets or is cantilievered. *See* CIBORIUM.

ballflower a medieval type of ornamentation, characteristic of the 14th century, in the form of a ball cupped by the three petals of a globular-shaped flower.

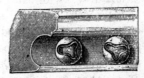

a hollow with ballflower ornamentation

baluster one of a series of short posts or pillars which make up a BALUSTRADE. The balusters support a rail at the top and stand on a base at the bottom. They may be constructed from worked, turned stone forming, for example, a PARAPET on the roof of a classical building or as part of an ornamental bridge. Staircases may have balustrades constructed from either wood or stone and may incorporate carved wood panelling and ironwork.

balustrade a series of BALUSTERS.

bargeboard or **vergeboard** projecting boards which are often carved and ornamented, placed on the verge of gables to conceal the ends of the horizontal roof timbers. The earliest known examples date from the 14th century and were often intricately carved and decorated.

barn a large building constructed for the storage of grain or hay and straw. Medieval barns were normally built of wood, but some large and important ones were constructed of stone and these usually belonged to a rich monastery or abbey and are known as abbey barns. Other large barns, known as tithe barns were constructed in medieval times to store the tithes levied from the population. This was a form of tax which was originally set at one tenth of everything produced. These large barns were designed like churches and divided into a nave and aisles, with buttressing. The roof was of timber frame construction and small windows provided ventilation for the stored produce. Surviving medieval examples include the abbey barn at Glastonbury, Somerset and one in Abbotsbury, Dorset.

baroque a form of classical architecture, mainly associated with the 17th and part of the18th century, with its origins in Italy. It is an exuberant and unrestrained form, dominated by the use of large, bold curves and the massing together of large shapes, with much decoration and ornamentation. It arose, after the Renaissance, from a need to turn back to spiritual values and the Roman Catholic faith, and particularly suited the Latin peoples of Southern Europe. The most famous artistic expoenents of Baroque were Gianlorenzo Bernini and Francesco Borromini. In its true form Baroque architecture was also popular in Spain, Portugal, Austria, Southern Germany, Czechoslovakia and Switzerland. In Northern Europe and Britain, the movement was short-lived (1690–1730) and was much more restrained by classical elements. Sir Christopher Wren in his designs at Greenwich; Sir John Vanburgh at Blenheim and Castle Howard, and Nicholas Hawkmoor at Christ Church, Spitalfields, brought their own personal interpretation to Baroque, also shown in the work of Thomas Archer. Their buildings are sometimes described as Baroque classicism to indicate the restraining influence of classical elements on the style in Britain.

barrel vault the simplest type of vault, used by the Romans and later in romanesque architecture, which is tunnel-shaped and is also known as a *tunnel* or *wagon* vault. A broad and pointed form of barrel vault was used in Romanesque buildings.

a barrel vault

base the part beneath the shaft of a COLUMN and the pavement or PEDESTAL. Early bases were relatively small and insignificant consisting of quarter-rounded moulding on a square plinth. Later, these became more substantial and continued to take a variety of forms, depending upon the architectural period. *See* CLASSICAL ORDER.

a Romanesque column base

basement the lowest storey of a building which is often completely or partially below ground level. It is more likely to be used as a living area rather than for storage (cf. CELLAR).

basilica one of the most important public buildings of a Roman city, used as a centre of commerce and a hall of justice and situated near the FORUM. The term describes its function rather than the style of the building, but the basilica was usually rectangular in plan and divided lengthwise by colonnades to form AISLES or GALLERIES flanking a large central area. Often there was one or more APSE. Early basilica usually had an open timber roof or a flat wood ceiling which might or might not be decorated. Later examples, especially the larger ones, had a vaulted roof supported by huge stone piers, e.g. the Basilica of Maxentius in Rome. Early Christian churches were built on a plan derived from the basilica.

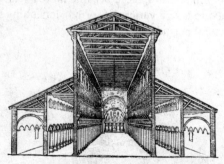

a typical basilica, illustrating colonnades

bastion a projecting part built out from the angle of a fortified building which allowed the occupants to view and defend the ground in front of the ramparts.

bastle a type of farmhouse, dating from 1650–1750, built along the remote, upland areas of the Scottish border and known as a bastel-house. It was usually vaulted, accommodating the farm animals at ground level and the family above, and could be defended against attack.

Bath stone a creamy-fawn coloured building stone quarried near Bath and used for buildings throughout the ages in and around the city.

batten a long, thin piece of rectangular-shaped timber supporting roof slates or tiles, or lath and plaster.

batter a sloping wall or inclined face as in a tower, wall or other surface that is wider at the bottom and narrower at the top.

battlement a PARAPET with indentations known as EMBRASURES or CRENELLES (crenellation) alternating with protrusions called MERLONS or COPS. The whole is finished with COPING. Battlements run along the top of the walls of fortified buildings dating from the Middle Ages and were for defensive purposes. Also, they were added as decorative features to later buildings such as town houses and the towers of churches.

bay a principal vertical division of the interior or exterior of a building marked by buttresses or pilasters, ribs of vaulting, by an order, compartments of the roof or fenestration. It is especially associated with church architecture.

bay window a window which projects out from the wall in semicircular, rectangular or polygonal shape, forming a recess within a room. If curved, i.e. semicircular in shape, it is called a bow window and if only on the upper storey of the building, an oriel window.

bay leaf garland a small moulding, cylindrical in shape and characteristic of the ROMANESQUE period, which is ornamented to look like a string of beads.

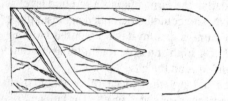

a typical bay leaf moulding

beakhead a decorative type of motif characteristic of the Norman period consisting of carved human, animal or bird heads with a beak often found in doorways. Another similar form, called Catshead has a protruding tongue instead of a beak.

beam a horizontal, transverse timber in the roof of a building. In between the floors of a building, beams are main horizontal supporting timbers for the JOISTS. A dragon beam projects diagonally out at the corner of a building. It provides support for the joists of a JETTY.

beehive construction an ancient type of one roomed dwelling house constructed out of a variety of materials in a beehive shape. Sardinia has some prehistoric examples known as *nuraghi*. Similar ancient buildings in Ireland and Scotland, but of a later date, were constructed from stones. Each course of stones was corbelled inwards and met at the top to form a vaulted structure. These are known as wheel-houses in Ireland and BROCHS in Scotland. Ancient cultures also used beehive construction for tombs, e.g. the Tholos tombs at Mycenae, Greece, the most famous being the Treasury of Atreus dating from 1330 BC. Houses of beehive construction which are still in use, called *Trulli* are still to be found in Greece.

belfry the word has its roots in the old French *berfrei* and English *berfray*, and originally applied to a movable tower used by those laying siege to a fortified town or castle. Later on, it was used to describe a watch tower or bell tower for sounding an alarm bell. Now, a belfry is the upper chamber in a church tower where the bells are housed, or the whole bell tower itself.

a belfry

bell tower a tower, either attached to, or separate from a church in which the bells are hung.

a Byzantine bell tower

belvedere derived from the Italian, *bel vedere*, meaning a view. This is an elevated turret on the top of a house constructed for obtaining a view. See also GAZEBO.

bema this has its origin in the Greek word for step, and in ancient Greece was an elevated platform from which an orator addressed an audience. In the Early Christian church, the bema was a similar platform or stage in the chancel or apse, which the clergyman mounted to preach to the congregation. In the Eastern

Byzantine church the bema is an elevated area containing the altar, behind the ICONOSTASIS. In the Jewish synagogue, the bema is the raised pulpit from which the Torah and Pentateuch are read, but its position within the building varies. Bema is also sometimes used to refer to the chancel in a church.

berm a feature of a barrow or hill fort describing the level area which separates the bank from the ditch.

béton brut concrete which is left in its natural unfinished state once the FORMWORK has been removed. It is also called board-marked concrete.

billet a type of Romanesque moulding, comprising rows of raised square or short cylindrical pieces arranged to form a pattern.

a typical billet moulding

bird's beak moulding a type of moulding used in the architecture of ancient Greece which, in section, resembles a bird's beak.

blind tracery also known as blank tracery, this is a characteristic feature of Gothic architecture and is the tracery work on wood panels or walls or surfaces other than windows.

blind window a false window where there is no opening. It was often used as a decoration in buildings from the Medieval period onwards, sometimes to confer symmetry on a FACADE.

blocking course either a plain course of stone or brick above a classical CORNICE on the top of a building; or a course of projecting stone or brick at the base of a building.

bolection moulding a projecting moulding which conceals the join between two surfaces at different levels.

bonnet tile also known as a cone or hip bonnet, a type of curved tile with a rounded top which joins with the plain tiles along the hip of the roof.

boss a projecting, rounded, carved and ornamental knob used on ceilings or vaults where stone ribs or wooden beams converged. It is often carved with a leaf pattern.

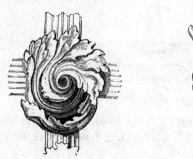

examples of decorative bosses

box a small country home or minor residence, e.g. a shooting box.

box-frame a form of concrete structure designed like a series of boxes one on top of the other where the cross walls carry the loads. Also called cross-wall construction, this type of building is suitable as office blocks, halls of residence, etc. where many similar units are repeated.

brace a secondary length of timber which may be either straight or curved and which is fixed diagonally to strengthen a roof or other structure.

bracket a generally small projection from a wall, constructed of stone, metal or wood used to support the weight of another structure such as a shelf, arch, cornice, statue or beam. A bracket is often highly decorated and ornamented, carved and shaped although may be plain.

brattishing a carved ornamental cresting on the top of a parapet, cornice or screen used in the late medieval period. Its most usual form is as leaves or flowers, sometimes battlemented.

bressumer the main horizontal beam, often carved or decorated in a timber-framed construction supporting a wall or projecting gable. It is also used to describe the beam supporting the lintel of a large fireplace or other wide opening.

bricks and **brickwork** bricks are rectangular blocks cut and shaped from a soft material such as mud or clay, and either allowed to dry and harden in the sun or fired at high temperatures in a kiln. Bricks have been used by Man for the construction of buildings for thousands of years. They are relatively simple to produce from raw material which is usually readily available, and can be made in different sizes. They are strong and can be used alone or with other types of stone (as in Roman walls), and provide good insulation. Bricks vary in texture and colour according to the type of clay used and the manufacturing process. In countries with hot climates, bricks were usually baked in the sun as in Egypt and Mesopotamia (*see* ADOBE). However, baking using some sort of firing process was also employed in the Near East by 3000 BC and in pre-Roman Britain. The Romans used brickwork for building very widely throughout the Empire. The bricks were used to provide bonding courses at regular intervals in walls, interspersed betwen other layers of masonry, rubble or flint. Roman bricks varied in size and shape depending upon their use. Those used for walls were somewhat flat and thin, resembling tiles, whereas those for floors were small rectangular blocks. Square bricks were used to construct underfloor piers or pilae and hollow box bricks were placed in walls, both as part of a building's heating system. In Roman Britain, bricks were very well-fired and many examples can still be seen. Also, they were extensively incorporated into later buildings once the Romans had left. Following the period of Roman occupation, the use of brickwork declined in Britain although not in other countries in Europe. Brickwork became popular once again in the Tudor period and from the 1630s onwards, classical features were skilfully executed using bricks. The technology for producing bricks improved and their versatility and decorative qualities came to be appreciated. The imposition of a brick tax in 1780, which was twice increased, made the cost of using bricks prohibitive for smaller buildings. However, this was repealed in 1850 and throughout the Victorian period, bricks were the commonest building material and were extensively used both for dwellings and in railway construction. Bricks are still extensively used today.

A stretcher is a brick which is laid sideways in a wall so that only the side is visible. A header is a brick laid lengthways so that only the end is visible in a wall. A section of a header is called a closer and is sometimes used to finish the open end of a wall. Closers have a variety of shapes which are given different names, e.g. bevelled, Queen, King. Various methods of laying bricks are given different names. Various rules are followed to provide strong bonding, the most important being to lay the bricks so that there are no continuous vertical joints. English bond describes a wall in which there are alternate layers (or courses) of headers and stretchers. English garden wall bond has three courses of stretchers and one of headers throughout the wall. Flemish bond has alternating stretchers and headers in each course throughout the wall. Heading bond has only headers throughout the wall. Brick-on-edge bond in which the bricks, which are normally headers, are laid on edge as in a sill. American bond is the same as English garden-wall bond. Brick-on-end bond in which stretchers are laid on end. Dutch bond, a type of English bond in which the courses of stretchers are moved half a brick to the left or right to produce a staggered pattern in the wall. English cross bond—a similar staggered pattern is produced but further exaggerated by the insertion of closers. Broken bond, in which the height or width of the wall does not allow for the sequence to be completed before it is interrupted by a door or window. The broken bond is placed in the centre of the wall in order to preserve the pattern. Dearne's bond, in which there are alternate courses of stretchers and headers throughout the wall with the stretchers laid on edge and the headers are laid flat or on bed. Flemish stretcher bond in which the Flemish bond pattern is interspersed by courses, (usually three), of stretchers alone. Flemish garden-wall bond, also known as Scotch and Sussex bond is a wall in which the Flemish bond has stretchers (usually three), between each header. Rat trap bond is a variation of Flemish bond in which all the bricks are laid on edge. Silver-lock's bond is the same as Rat trap bond but only the stretchers are laid on edge. Both provide a method of forming cavities in the wall. Racking bond is a type used at the base or in walls which are very thick. Irregular bond in which there is no set bonding pattern but the vertical joints are broken to preserve strength. Monk bond is another variation of Flemish bond, also known as Flying Flemish bond, in which two stretchers are placed between each header. Stretcher bond uses only stretchers throughout a cavity wall. Stock bond in which the bricks are laid on end and there are unbroken vertical joints. Herring bond brickwork is a type of bonding in which there is a diagonal pattern with the bricks meeting at right angles in a V shape. The brickwork which fills in the spaces between the timbers in a building of timber-frame construction, is called nogging. Honeycomb brickwork is a type of walling in which some bricks are omitted, either to provide ventilation or as a decorative feature.

bridge a construction built across a natural obstacle such as a river or gorge or a man-made one such as a railway, canal or road. The four main types are a) arch bridge in which one or more arches provide the support; b) suspension bridge in which the whole structure is hung from a high framework at either side, e.g. Clifton Suspension

Bridge, Bristol; c) girder bridge in which the structure is carried by supports at either end; and d) cantilever bridge. Movable bridges are usually built across rivers to allow passage of shipping beneath. There are three main types: swing bridge which swings away horizontally; bascule bridge, the two halves of which move vertically, e.g. Tower Bridge, London; and drawbridge.

Stone and wood were the main construction materials for the early bridges and the oldest large example, dating from 219 BC is at Martorell in Spain. Iron bridges were constructed in Britain from the late 1700s. Famous names associated with bridge building include George and Robert Stephenson and Isambard Kingdom Brunel.

broch *see* **beehive**

building block a block of material used for construction, e.g. a brick or block of precast concrete.

bungalow a single storey detached dwelling house. Bungalow is derived from an Indian word *banglā*, which described the type of house with verandah given to English officials in the rural parts of India in the mid 1800s.

buttress a projecting mass of brickwork or masonry built out from a wall as a support. Buttresses are usually needed to counteract the weight and lateral thrust of the roof, especially when this is of arched or stone vault construction. However, they are also required when openings such as windows take away strength from the wall. Buttresses are often associated with large buildings such as churches. In Saxon and Norman construction, thick walls were built which required less support so that buttresses tend to be wide but with a low projection. When Gothic architecture developed, buildings were constructed with thinner walls, large windows and vaulting of ribbed stone, and with a greater need for strong buttresses of larger projection. These buttresses were made deeper at the base but diminishing and becoming thinner at intervals towards the roof. These intervals or stages are marked by shaping or moulding and at the top by a pinnacle or other carved shape. There are various types of buttress:

1. Angle buttress—two buttresses which meet at a 90º angle at the corner of the building. This type of design was commonly used from the 1200s onwards.

2. Clasping buttress—a less frequently used, large, square type of buttress which clasps or encases the angle of the building. It is usually built around a tower or porch.

3. Diagonal buttress—a type of buttress set diagonally against the right angle made where two walls meet, often of a tower.

4. Lateral buttress—a type of buttress built at the angle of a building on the same axis as one of the walls.

5. Setback buttress—similar to the angle buttress but the two buttresses, instead of meeting at right angles, are set back slightly so that the corner of the building protrudes between them.

6. Flying buttress—also known as an arch buttress, in which an arch or part of an arch carries the thrust of a roof of vault, from the upper part of the wall to an outer buttress. Flying buttresses developed along with Gothic architecture and were a necessary means of diverting the pressure exerted by roof vaulting down to the ground and away from the building. Heavy pinnacles on top of the buttresses also helped to counteract the thrust exerted by the vaulting.

a section of Cologne Cathedral, illustrating flying butresses

Byzantine architecture a style of architecture associated
with the Byzantine empire which reached its highest
point of influence, governing lands stretching from the
Danube to the Euphrates, in the middle of the 6th century
AD. The Imperial Centre of Government was transferred
to Byzantium from Rome in AD 330 by Constantine, the
Roman Emperor. The small city of Byzantium (later
Constantinople and now Istanbul), on the river
Bosphorus, had existed since 666 BC but now a much
grander capital was planned. Later in the 4th century, the
Roman Empire was divided into two, with Byzantium as
the capital of the eastern part. The western empire eventually fell leaving Byzantium as the only remaining capital city. The architecture, while initially drawn from the
classical styles of Rome and Greece, soon became influenced by the eastern worlds of Persia, Armenia and
Syria. During the 6th century this had developed into a
distinctive form of its own influencing the style and
decoration of buildings in many countries. The Byzantine style is mainly to be seen in churches and monastic
buildings and less is known about the domestic architecture. A distinctive form of architecture had evolved by
the 6th century, combining features based on the basilican plan and the Greek cross plan (called the Martyria).
Classical orders and decoration became less prominent
and the ornamentation tended to be rather flat and lacy.
Brick became the main building material with the use of
marble and mosaics internally instead of carved decoration. Roofs were domed and exteriors rather plain, using
simple terracotta decorations or marble facing. Inside a
Byzantine church there is an atmosphere of mystery, a

section of the Church at St Sophia at Constantinople

playing of light and shade. Narrow beams of light from small windows reflect off the mosaic decoration to create a glimmering effect. Wide curving surfaces were decorated with beautifully executed mosaic pictures telling the story of Christianity using vivid colours and gold. An example of an early Byzantine church is that of Hagia Sophia, Istanbul (AD 532-7) and a later one is St. Marks Cathedral in Venice. The Byzantine style persisted until the 13th century influencing church building in many different countries. Byzantine themes were used by architects in Britain in later years, for example by John Francis Bentley in Westminster Cathedral.

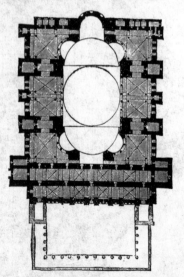

ground-plan of the Church of St Sophia at Constantinople

C

cable moulding a type of Romanesque moulding resembling a twisted rope.

caisson a word derived from the French meaning locker or large chest. A foundation structure used for construction in waterlogged ground or below water as in the building of a bridge. It is a chamber driven into firm ground below the construction, which provides a water-tight air chest. Sunken panels in a ceiling or vault.

caliduct a pipe for carrying hot air, steam or water as part of a heating system.

camber a horizontal roof timber which is usually either a collar beam or tie beam, with ends lower than the centre, conferring a shallow convex curve. (*See* ROOF).

campanile a type of bell tower which is normally separate from the church building.

a campanile

45

campus a group of buildings sited in parkland, and often situated in the country, which are used by students and scholars in an academic community. The first university campus was started in 1806 and the concept has remained popular until the present day.

cancelli a grille or lattice screen in early Christian churches which divided the choir from the main part of the building.

canopy a hood either suspended from a ceiling or projecting out from a wall as a covering for an altar, pulpit, statue, tomb, niche, window, door, etc, which may be of carved wood, stone or other material.

canopy of the tomb of Cardinal d'Amboise at Rouen

cantilever a shaped, horizontal projection such as a girder, beam, step or bracket which is strongly secured by a downward force behind a fulcrum at one end. The free end or the whole length of the structure carries a load. The cantilever principle is used in the construction of bridges, steps and for brackets supporting a large balcony or cornice.

capital the head of a pilaster or column which is larger than the column itself and often highly carved, moulded and decorated. The capital provides a large surface to support an ARCH or ENTABLATURE and is also an ornamental feature. The top part is a flat slat called the ABACUS and beneath this is a narrower part called the NECKING. A moulding usually marks the division between the necking and the shaft of the column. The form and style of the column capital varies according to the form of architecture, *see* CLASSICAL ORDER. Some common types of capital are:

1. Bell—in the form of an upside down bell, a type used in Classical and Gothic architecture.

bell style capital in the Temple at Edfu

2. Cushion or block or cube—shaped and moulded from a cube but with the lower portion cut and rounded to fit the column. A flat face is left above on each of the four sides and this is called a lunette. This type of capital is typical of Romanesque, Norman and BYZANTINE forms.

cushion style capital in the Cathedral of Limburg on the Lahn

3. Basket capital—another typical Byzantine form, roughly in the shape of a hemisphere and intricately and deeply carved to give a wicker-work effect resembling a basket. The types of pattern used include scrolls, leaves and circular shapes. Byzantine capitals often have a large block on top of the ABACUS which is called a DOSSERET or *pulvino*.

*basket style capital from the Church of
St Sophia at Constantinople*

4. Scalloped—developed from the cushion capital where the lunettes are carved into cone shapes.

scalloped capital in the Cathedral at Spires

5. Palm—a form from ancient Egypt shaped like the crown of a palm tree.

6. Lotus—another ancient Egyptian form with the crown shaped like a lotus bud.

7. Protomai—a type of capital with carved figures, generally of animals, protruding from its four corners.

8. Foliated—typical of Gothic architecture and showing various forms. The *Crocket* is carved in the form of stylized leaves ending in classical VOLUTES. The stiff-leat, typical of the 12th and 13th century in Britain with sculptured leaves and the water leaf with broad, plain leaves curving over towards the abacus. *See also* CLASSICAL ORDER.

foliated capital at Cologne Cathedral

carrel also known as a carol, a small niche in the cloister of a monastery where a monk would sit and meditate or work.

cartouche a kind of shield-shaped ornament, often carved in the form of an heraldic device or with lettering, and enclosed in scrolls representing rolls of paper.

caryatid a carved female figure used like a column to support an overlying structure or ENTABLATURE. Similar male figures are called *Atlantes* (singular, *Atlas*) or *telamones*, and female figures carrying a basket on their head are called *canophorae*. Human figures of three-quarter length which emerge from a pedestal are called Herms while similar mythical or animal figures are called Terms. These are often found on either side of an 18th century fireplace in a grand house.

a caryatid from a Greek temple

casement either a type of wide, concave, hollow moulding found in window and door jambs; or, a type of opening of a window with hinges fastened to the vertical part of the outside frame.

castle a fortified dwelling or group of buildings, occupied in times of danger by the lord of the manor and all those dependent upon him. The early castles were constructed of wood based on the MOTTE-AND-BAILEY plan. The motte was either a natural hill or mound or one which was built from earth, with a deep ditch excavated all the way round the base. The castle was built on top of the motte, and was occupied by the lord and his family and retainers, and it was protected by an encircling wooden fence. Beyond this there was an area of land, the bailey, also protected by a wooden fence. Beyond the fence a rampart of earth was constructed surrounded at its base by another deep ditch, known as a fosse. Often, a stream was diverted to fill the fosse with water. The bailey was occupied by a variety of buildings, e.g. store houses, cottages, stables, soldiers' quarters, barns, smithy and bakehouse, the number depending upon the size and importance of the castle. Fortified bridges, which could be easily defended, crossed the ditches along the route leading to the castle. At times of danger, everyone lived within the bailey or castle and the whole could be defended with the occupants self-sufficient enough to be able to endure a siege. This type of structure was usual after the Roman occupation up until about 1100. After this time, especially with the larger and more important castles, stone was used for building, replacing the earlier wooden constructions. These are known as keeps or *donjons* and were of two types; the shell keeps which were less strong and Norman keeps built on a rectangular plan. Shell keeps were built on as motte and had walls around 20–25 feet high and 8–10 feet thick. The walls were of rubble with QUOINS (shaped stones) at the corners and with a PLINTH (projecting base) of ASHLAR. Stone and timber buildings were constructed within the walls and the whole was usually constructed on a polygonal or circular plan. Remains of shell keeps are found at a number of sites, e.g. Berkeley castle and Cardiff castle, sometimes with later re-building.

The massive rectangular Norman keeps, built in Britain on the French donjon plan, were vast, immensely strong constructions. Due to their size and mass, they had to be constructed on solid foundations and were too heavy for an artificial motte. A natural area of higher ground within the bailey was usually chosen on which to build the keep, with use being made of cliffs and other natural barriers. The walls were very thick, especially at the splayed base where they could be as much as 20 feet, reaching a height of 100 feet. Flat BUTTRESSES at the corners and in the middle of each of the four sides provided further support for the building. Turrets were built at the corner with a spiral stone staircase in each running from top to bottom throughout all four or five floor levels. Rooms of various sorts and garderobes for sanitation, were built within the walls, as were chimneys and fireplaces. The basement was used for storage and often contained the dungeons. The main living area, which was the great hall, was built on the first floor and could be as much as 30 feet high and 45 feet square. In large halls such as this, a stone dividing wall with arches was needed to support the structure and the ceiling provided a floor for the storey above. On this second floor the apartments of the lord and his family, and the chapel in larger castles, were usually to be found. On the floor above there was a roof with the BATTLEMENTS on which kitchens were situated. During times of siege, the fires and ovens were used for the preparation of missiles. The main entrance into the castle was protected by a tower and the inner doors were massive oak structures usually preceded by a drawbridge and PORTCULLIS. A fine example of a Norman keep is the White Tower or the Tower of London.

The massive Norman keeps were constructed entirely as defensive structures and by the middle of the 13th century, there was a need for castles from which offensive military operations could be mounted. Hence the plan of castles underwent a change and these later constructions are known as Edwardian (after Edward I), or concentric castles. These had three rings of walls, interrupted at intervals by fortified towers, one inside the other and less thick than those of the Norman keeps. A moat surrounded the outer wall with the entrance defended by a gatehouse. Sometimes another type of outer defensive structure with towers, called a barbican, was constructed to protect the inner gatehouse. Inside the inner ring of walls, separate buildings were constructed rather than a keep, such as the chapel, great hall and living apartments. Other buildings and accommodation for soldiers, retainers and stables were constructed within the outer rings of walls. A good example of a concentric castle is Beaumaris Castle on Anglesey. Sometimes, the Norman keeps were adapted to the concentric plan. Some later castles were built as part of the defences of a town on a rather different plan, e.g. Conway and Caernarvon.

Eventually, the need for massive fortified structures became less great and more emphasis was placed on the comfort of living quarters. Large castles were sometimes converted to palaces and smaller ones became fortified country houses.

Gothic castle which copies the style of the middle ages

castrum a Roman army camp based on a rectangular plan. The outer boundary of the camp was a defensive RAMPART and wall with towers positioned along its length. Two roadways, the *decumanus* and *cardo* crossed the camp leading to a gateway in each of the four sides. These gates were called the *porta decumana*, *porta praetoria*, *porta sinistra* and *porta dextra*. In the centre where the two roads crossed lay the military headquarters or *praetorium*. The other military buildings such as the armoury and barracks were sited in the four corners divided off by the roadways.

cast stone also known as reconstructed stone, this is a type of building material made from an aggregate of various types of natural stone which is cemented together. It is used in the same way as solid stone and is often faced with stone of a different type. Many types of cast stone have been in use for many hundreds of years and have proved to be strong and hard-wearing building material.

catacomb a cemetery constructed underground, often on several levels. The word applied to early Christian cemeteries (before the 6th century) in and near Rome, Sicily, North Africa and Naples. These were variable in plan but generally had underground galleries linked together which opened out into chambers (*cubicula*), with niches (*arcosolia*) and shelves (*loculi*) for tombs. The walls of the galleries and chambers were often painted with religious scenes. Catacombs were rarely used for Christian burials after the 6th century, and the word is now applied to any underground cemeteries, including those of other religions.

cathedra the bishop's throne or special chair of state in a cathedral church, normally situated in the APSE behind the high altar.

cathedral the principal church of a diocese presided over by a bishop and containing his official throne. The word is derived from CATHEDRA.

view of the Cathedral at Pisa

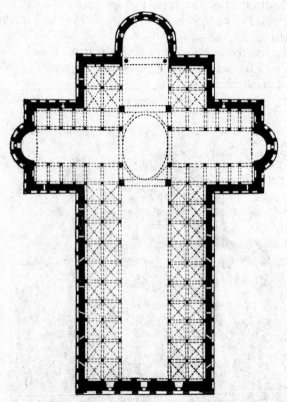

ground-plan of the Cathedral at Pisa

cavetto moulding a type of hollowed-out concave moulding about a quarter of a circle in section.

cella the main area of a classical temple containing the
statue or image of the deity.

cellar a storage room wholly or partly below ground.

cement a type of binding substance which may be the natural material holding, for example, the grains of a rock together as in the matrix of a sandstone. Or, it may be a manufactured chemical substance, to which water is added and used wet, that dries and sets hard to bind building materials together.

cenotaph a monument built in honour of a person or many persons who have died and are buried elsewhere. It is usually associated with those who have fallen in war as a memorial and place of remembrance.

chair rail also known as a DADO RAIL, a wooden moulding running around the walls of a room at chair back height. Its purpose is to prevent damage to the wall if chairs are pushed back.

chamfer a flat surface created when the sharp edge where two sides of a rectangular block of wood or stone meet at right angles (ARRIS), is cut away. The flat surface is usually at a 45° angle to the two faces of the block. If the cut surface is further hollowed out to form a concave curve, it is termed a hollow chamfer. If it is cut to form one or more rows of convex mouldings, it is called a moulded chamfer. A sunk chamfer is one in which the surface is flat but sunk farther down than normal. A stopped or stop chamfer is one in which the surface does not continue along the full length of the beam or stone block. It finishes in a carved splay ending in a point where the two surfaces of the block once more meet to form the edge or ARRIS.

chancel an area within a church, situated at the east end and containing the altar, which is occupied by the choir and clergy. The word is derived from the Latin *cancellus* which, strictly-speaking, applied to the screen that usually separated this area from the rest of the church.

chantry chapel a small chapel, either inside a larger church or attached to it, where mass was said for the soul of the founder. Chantry chapels were often beautifully decorated and ornate.

chapel a room or small building set aside and dedicated for Christian worship. From medieval times onwards, a chapel for private worship was an important place in the home of a lord or nobleman and in public institutions such as schools, universities, military garrisons, hospitals and prisons.

Large churches and cathedrals may contain one or more chapels, the most important being the Lady Chapel in honour of the Virgin Mary. Some cathedrals contain a Royal chapel in which the tomb of a monarch is situated, e.g. that of Henry VII in Westminster Abbey. Roadside chapels, known as chapels of ease were also sometimes built in the Middle Ages for the use of people who were travelling.

chapterhouse the governing body of a monastery or cathedral church, which is responsible for the everyday running of all aspects of the establishment or community, is known as the Chapter. The Chapterhouse is the building where the members of the Chapter meet for the discussion and administration of business. In a monastery it was usually reached from the CLOISTERS and usually had a polygonal plan in Britain. It contained rows of canopied seats and several fine examples exist, e.g. in Wells Cathedral.

charnel house a room in which bodies were kept often as

part of a CHANTRY CHAPEL, derived from the old French *charnel* meaning burial place.

chase a narrow channel dug into a floor or wall for the housing of pipes, cables or conduits, which is later infilled with mortar and finished externally.

chequer work a type of decorative pavement or wall using alternate squares of different materials to produce a chequer board pattern. From the 1400s–1600s, alternate squares of stone and knapped flint were commonly used.

chevron a type of Romanesque moulding in a zig-zag pattern.

typical chevron mouldings on Romanesque columns

chimney originally this described the fireplace or hearth but later it came to include the flue, the chimney breast which houses the flue, and the exit stacks for smoke on the roof of the building. True chimneys were rarely built before the 14th century. Usually, the most important living area or great hall had a central fireplace or hearth and smoke escaped through a hole or louvre in the roof. At the end of the 13th century fireplaces were built in more rooms and on outside walls. Flues were built through the thick walls and the smoke escaped via an outlet only a short distance from the fireplace itself. Later, flues were constructed vertically through the thick walls of a castle or other building and smoke escaped through a chimney shaft on the roof.

From being purely functional structures in the earlier years of the Middle Ages, fireplaces and chimney pieces became increasingly important as ornamental features in later centuries. The fireplace was often the most significant ornamental feature within a room and was often highly decorative and ornate. Also, in the first half of the 6th century, chimney shafts and stacks became important decorative features on the exterior of a building. Different designs and patterns were achieved using coloured brickwork and terracotta. The advent of central heating has made the fireplace and chimney piece of lesser importance today than in the past.

Chimney bar—the lintel bar across and above the opening of the fireplace which supports the front of the chimney breast.

Chimney breast—a structure built of stone or brick which projects into the room and houses the flue.

Chimney piece or mantelpiece—the framework of wood, stone or brick surrounding a fireplace.

Chimney shaft—a structure on top of a roof containing one flue through which smoke is dispersed to the outside.

Chimney stack—larger structure on top of a building containing a number of flues.

Chimney pots—structures on top of shafts or stacks made of pottery or metal.

ciborium a CANOPY set over the high altar in a church.

circus a Roman circus was a building with long sides and rounded ends. It had tiers of seats at either side and around one end. In the 18th century, a development of houses built on a circular plan, and in the present day a circular road.

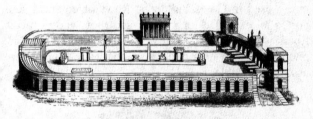

a Roman circus

citadel a fortress with four to six BASTIONS which defended and commanded a city. The citadel was often sited on higher ground, with the town developing round about.

cladding a covering or skin applied to the external surfaces of a building for protective and decorative purposes.

clapboard *see* **weatherboard**

classical architecture refers to the style of building of the ancient Greek civilization and later of the Romans. The architecture of ancient Greece developed over a period of about 200 years reaching its highest point of refinement about 550 BC. The style was simple and limited in its form and variety, but with infinite attention paid to the line and proportions of buildings. The aim was to produce buildings which looked absolutely aesthetically correct, and in order to achieve this enormous attention was paid to detail with refinements of line, curve and mass. Buildings which survive from this period include temples, public buildings of various kinds and theatres. They were built in the post-and-lintel or trabeated style (from the Latin word *trabes* meaning a beam), based on vertical supports which were columns, carrying horizontal beams or lintels or marble or stone. Arches and vaults were rarely used in Greek buildings. Rows of columns supported an extended long lintel, and roofs and porticos. Roofs were usually constructed of wood and had a low pitch, with tiles of terracotta or marble. Ceilings were usually of marble.

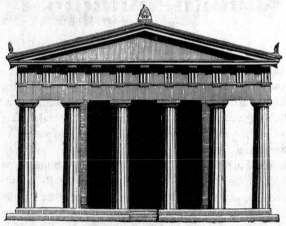

front of a Greek Temple

The Greeks developed the system of orders (*see* CLAS-SICAL ORDER) in which each part was perfectly proportioned and calculated to fit with the rest. They became aware that a true vertical or horizontal line appears concave when seen by the human eye, especially if viewed against the skyline of a bright blue, cloudless sky. To counteract this, Greek architects developed precisely calculated, slightly convex lines (which are curves of parabolas rather than arcs of circles) so that buildings appeared visually correct. The finest example of this is the Parthenon in Athens where these fine adjustments have been made to all the vertical and horizontal lines of the building. Similar refinements were made to the width and spacing of the columns in order to achieve perfection of form and line. As these adjustments had to be very accurately calculated, they were costly to produce and were reserved for the most important buildings.

In the earlier years of Greek civilization, the main building materials were bricks dried in the sun, stone, terracotta and wood. Later, marble came to be used for all important buildings. If it was not possible to use marble, a type of stucco manufactured from powdered white marble was applied to the external surfaces of buildings. The use of colour was widely employed for decorative purposes, both on the interior and exterior of buildings. The blocks of stone or marble were so finely and precisely cut that joins were almost invisible and there was little need for mortar. Dowels and cramps of metal were more usually employed to hold the blocks together.

The Romans continued to build in the trabeated Greek style, but adapted and extended it in various ways to suit their particular needs. There was an increasing use of arches and vaults and less reliance on the precise placing

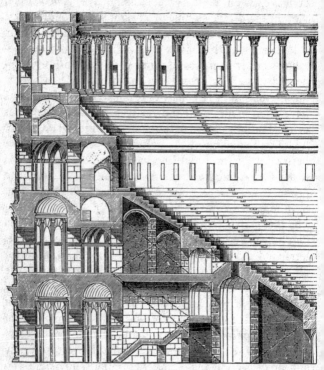

section of the Colosseum at Rome

of columns and lintels. This enabled them to construct buildings with more storeys than those built by the Greeks. The Romans continued to use the orders but with further additions of their own. Often a different order was used on each storey as in the Colosseum in Rome. Mouldings and ornaments were more abundant and less refined than those of the Greeks. Early buildings were usually constructed of brickwork often faced with concrete, stucco and later, marble. The Romans produced an extremely strong and hard-wearing form of concrete, based on a volcanic ash called pozzolana, available near Rome and Naples. It made possible the construction of massive buildings, the best surviving example being the Pantheon in Rome. From the early days of the Roman empire onwards, marble was increasingly in demand for buildings and it was imported from far afield. When marble was not available marble stucco was used as facing on brick and concrete buildings.

classical order the system of orders was first invented by the ancient Greeks and further enlarged and adapted by the Romans. It continued to influence architecture throughout the centuries almost until the present day. The order is a grouping together of certain structural parts, the proportions and ornament of these being determined by precise rules and requirements. The order consists of a vertical COLUMN usually resting on a BASE, with a SHAFT, CAPITAL and ENTABLATURE. The entablature is the horizontal part or lintel, itself divided into an ARCHITRAVE at the base, a central FRIEZE and an upper CORNICE.

The Greeks developed three orders which were arrived at by experimentation over quite a long period of time. These were the Greek Doric, Greek Ionic and Greek Corinthian, and usually only one was used for the exterior of a building (although a different one might be used in the interior). The Doric was the order most commonly used on the mainland of Greece, with the Ionic tending to be employed in the eastern lands of Asia Minor and the Aegean islands. In all the Greek orders, the shafts of the columns are carved out and fluted.

Greek Doric Order—the most popular and carefully devised of the Greek orders. The columns are closely placed and lack bases, standing directly on the stylobate, a type of platform. The column shafts are shallowly fluted, with the number of flutes varying according to the type of building. The flutes are divided by ARRISES. The columns are usually thicker in older buildings, and their total height, including the capital, is between four and six and a half times the diameter at the base. The capital consists of a flat, square abacus beneath which is a curved, convex moulding called an echinus. Beneath this are further mouldings in the form of small, narrow rings (annular rings) or annulets above the NECKING. Beneath the necking, and between it and the shaft of the column, there is a groove called the hypotrachelium. The lowest member of the entablature, the architrave, is plain and above it is a narrow moulding called the tenia. The frieze in the Doric order is divided into blocks called triglyphs with spaces in between them called metopes. The triglyphs are carved vertically with grooves called glyphs and usually there is one triglyph over each column and one in between. The metopes were rectangular in shape in earlier buildings but square in later ones, and normally occupied by sculptured figures. Below each triglyph there is a moulding called the regulus carved into small projections called guttae. The cornice at the top of the entablature is plain, flat and projects outwards. On its undersurface or soffit, there are flat, square, projecting blocks called mutules arranged so that one lies over each triglyph and one lies in between. These have three rows of six guttae projecting from them.

Greek Ionic Order—a graceful order of smaller proportions than the Doric,

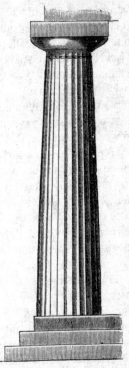

a Greek Doric column

and also of later origin. The columns are thinner and the shafts are carved into 24 half-circular flutes divided by FILLETS. The columns are set on bases which are usually carved. Commonly, these are attic bases, a type which has two large convex rings of moulding, the lower greater in size than the upper, separated by a wide concave moulding. The capital has a pair of scrolls known as volutes, a form of carving in the shape of curved shells or animal horns. Beneath this is a type of moulding known as echinus, decorated with EGG-AND-DART ornament. The entablature is usually one fifth of the whole order and so narrower than in the Doric. The architrave has a surface in three planes, set one on top of the other and each projecting farther outwards towards the top. The frieze is usually ornamented with sculpture in a continuous band all the way round and there are no triglyphs or metopes. The cornice is less projecting than in the Doric order with a small block type of ornament known as a dentil. The upper part of the cornice, known as the co-

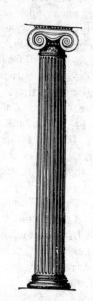

a Greek Ionic column

rona, is a projection with a vertical face and this is surmounted by a type of moulding called cyma recta (or OGEE). The order was more often used for the interiors of buildings or smaller constructions and in Asia Minor.
Greek Corinthian Order—an order developed in the 5th century Athens which was used much less frequently than the other two orders, hence fewer examples survive. The entablature is usually highly decorated with a deep

cornice. The capital has an abacus with four faces and beneath this, the shape resembles a concave bell decorated with acanthus leaf ornament. Variations on the theme of this capital, usually simpler forms, also occur in the Greek Corinthian order. However, this order really came into its own during the period of the Roman Empire when it was greatly developed and adapted.

Roman order—the Romans continued to use the Greek orders but modified and adapted them, and also developed two forms of their own.

Roman Doric Order—this is less substantial than the Greek Doric with thinner columns which have a base. Bulls' skulls wearing garlands usually replace the Greek metopes in the frieze. The mouldings and decoration are, in general, less refined than those of the Greek, with a plainer capital.

section of a Roman Doric column

Tuscan Order—an order evolved by the Romans based on Etruscan architecture. It was a simple and plain form and column shafts were rarely or never fluted. The height of the column was usually six times the diameter at the base. The entablature was simple, without ornamentation and the capital had a square abacus. The Tuscan order is considered to be a Roman variation of the Greek Doric. There are no existing remains from Roman times although the order was revived by some Renaissance architects.

section of a Tuscan Order column

Roman Ionic Order—this order was very similar to the Greek Ionic but more richly ornamented and embellished.

Roman Corinthian Order—an order based on the Greek design but further modified and adapted by the Romans, especially in the capital. Column shafts were either plain or fluted and the capital bell was highly ornamented with acanthus leaf design.

Roman Composite Order—an order evolved by the Romans combining elements of the Corinthian and Ionic. The main difference was in the capital in the type of decoration and moulding that was used. The order was richly decorated and was especially used for very ornate constructions such as triumphal arches.

classical ornament the same high degree of refinement and precision which the Greeks used in the construction of their buildings was employed in their ornament. Each part of a building, order or moulding had its own particular type of ornament which were beautifully and precisely executed to enhance the symmetry and aesthetic quality of the whole. The Greeks based their ornament on stylized animal and plant designs drawn from many countries and cultures—Minoan, Egyptian, Mycenean or Assyrian. The use of gold and colour was used to enrich the detail of the carvings. Animal designs used included the griffin, sphinx and lion head while among the plant forms were honeysuckle anthemion), acanthus leaf of the spiky spinosus type, and palm or palmette. BEAD-and-reel, EGG-AND-DART, BAY LEAF GARLAND, LEAF-AND-DART, dentil, SCROLL, FRET and GUILLOCHE ornaments were among those used on mouldings.

The Romans used similar ornaments but in a bolder, more free and less precise way. The acanthus leaf was of the rounded *Acanthus mollis* variety. Also, they used designs based on the leaves of the vine, olive, ivy and water lily and animals and birds taken from mythology. The use of garlands and bulls' skull ornament was commonly used, especially on Doric friezes.

an acanthus leaf moulding

classicism revivals of classical art and architecture which occurred at various times throughout European history. These revivals began in the Renaissance period, when there was a conscious attempt to arrive at a theory of classical architecture, based on the writings of VITRUVIUS. This theory was derived from ancient Roman buildings rather than those of Greece. This was because during the Renaissance, it was widely believed that the Roman civilization was the foundation of classical art and architecture and it was considered to be of far greater importance.

cloister an open space, usually in the form of a quadrangle, which is surrounded on all sides by AMBULATORIES, or roofed or vaulted passage ways.

cloister vault *see* **domical vault**.

cloisters in the monastery at Zurich

Coade stone a type of artificial stone fired in a kiln and composed of a combination of china clay, fluxes, sand and grog (finely ground fired stoneware particles). It was devised and developed in 1769 by Mr. & Mrs. George Coade but the business was further expanded, and continued to be successfully run, by their daughter Eleanor (1709-96) in Lambeth, London. The end material was a type of very hard and weather-resistant stoneware which was in great demand for ornament and sculpture. It was used by all the leading architects of the time including Adam, Soane, Chambers, Wyatt and Nash. Coade stone continued to be in demand until mid-Victorian times when it was gradually replaced by other materials. Many examples of work in Coade stone can still be seen, e.g. at Culzean Castle, Ayrshire; Buckingham Palace, London and Liverpool Town Hall.

coffering, coffer a type of ceiling decoration consisting of sunken panels, usually square, octagonal, hexagonal or diamond-shaped. Also called caissons or lacunae (*see* LACUNAR), these were highly decorated and ornamented in Roman and Renaissance architecture. Coffering was used in vaults, domes and ceilings, a Roman example from the 4th century AD being the Basilica of Maxentius.

colonnade a row of columns supporting ARCHES or ENTAB-LATURE.

column an upright, vertical support, with a circular cross-section used in many types of building and architectural styles from Classical times onwards. Columns were used in various ways, usually with others as a support but sometimes singly as a monument. In CLASSICAL ARCHITEC-TURE a column is usually made up of a base, shaft and capital and the diameter of the shaft is normally greater at the bottom, tapering towards the top. A blocked column has alternating cylindrical portions and rectangular blocks. An applied, engaged or attached column has part of its surface attached or arising from a wall. If it is a half or demi-column, only half the column protrudes from the surface of the wall. A compound, grouped or clustered pier is a feature of Gothic architecture in which a number of slender columns surround a central pier. These may be used as a decorative feature and banded at top, bottom or halfway up. This is known as annulated or banded. A type of column popular in Baroque architecture is a twisted form called the SOLOMONIC column. A type of Roman column which continued to be popular is the *columna rostrata* in which the decoration is of the prows of ships. It was used for the commemoration of victories at sea.

columination a building in which columns are used. Intercolumination refers to the spacing between columns.

composite construction a building component made of two or several different types of material.

concrete a type of building material, in use since ancient times, which is composed of a combination of sand, cement, stone and water that is used wet when it can be easily worked and moulded. It sets and dries, undergoing chemical changes, and becomes a rock-hard, durable, weather-resistant material. In ancient times, the cement which was used was not very strong and so the concrete has tended not to survive. The oldest example known dates from around 5600 BC. The Romans experimented with and further developed the use of concrete. A breakthrough came with the use of a volcanic ash called pozzolana from the area near Vesuvius and the town of Pozzuoli. It contained silica and aluminium and, when combined with lime, produced an extremely tough, hard-wearing concrete, the importance of which was soon realized by the Roman builders. It enabled them to construct more massive buildings than had been possible before, and its use continued in Europe for hundreds of years. In Britain, a satisfactory substitute using powdered brick and lime was successfully employed in such constructions as Hadrian's Wall. At the end of the Roman period in Britain, the use of concrete declined. It tended to be used as a foundation material or as infilling in the walls of churches and castles as in Salisbury Cathedral, dating from the 13th century. In the 18th and 19th centuries there was a renewed interest in developing a strong and durable cement like the Roman pozzolana. An English engineer, John Smeaton, carried out various experiments and discovered that lime derived from limestone which contained quantities of clay achieved the best results. This was used in his construction of the Eddystone lighthouse in 1750 which withstood the battering of seas and weather for over 100 years. Later, a French engineer, Louis J. Vicat (1786-1861) experimented with the chemical elements to make artificial cements, and James Frost, working in England, patented his British Cement in 1822. In 1824 an English bricklayer called Joseph Aspdin produced a superior product which he called Portland cement. This was later improved on and modified until in 1856 a product more closely resembling that used today was achieved. Its production required burning at high temperatures and was very costly. In the second half of the 19th century the use of concrete was hindered to a certain extent by the high costs of cement production, especially in the necessary grinding of the clinker and in the design of kilns. Eventually, advances in technology enable concrete to become the universal building material which it is today.

Reinforced concrete. Concrete reinforced with metal,

concrete

usually iron or steel, in the form of wires, bars or cables. This type enhances the naturally great compression resistance of the concrete to produce a building material of enormous strength. The Romans carried out some experiments in concrete reinforcement, with bronze as the metal which was used, but this was not found to work very well. It was in the late 18th and 19th centuries that experimentation with and use of reinforced concrete really began. In Europe, France led the way in the use of reinforced concrete followed later by Germany, Austria and also America. Development in Britain was somewhat slower but the first high-rise building using reinforced concrete was constructed in Liverpool in 1908.

Pre-stressed concrete. Concrete containing steel cables fed through ducts which are stretched and pulled before the concrete is cast into position. This induces compression stresses in the areas of the concrete which will later be loaded, making it stronger and less likely to crack. It results in the economical and efficient use of the concrete and the creation of more refined and slender forms of construction.

In the 1950s and 1960s, there was a tremendous expansion in the number of buildings constructed from pre-stressed concrete, e.g. high-rise flats. However, by the 1970s it was realized that the surfaces of buildings deteriorated and weathered rather badly, and now greater attention is paid to this problem. For many types of construction pre-stressed concrete remains unsurpassed and can be made to look attractive in its own right or when faced with marble, stone or mosaic.

Precast concrete. Concrete structures which are cast before being placed in position, either in a factory or at the construction site.

coping a covering of capping stones on the top of a wall, in the form of shaped slabs which are designed in various ways to allow for the run off of rainwater.

corbel a block which is usually made of stone, brick or wood which projects out from a surface as a support for an arch, beam, moulding, parapet or statue. A corbel-table is a row of corbels which support a battlement or parapet, as in Norman castles and Romanesque architecture. This may also be known as a corbel course. If corbel courses are built out so that each projects beyond the one below, this is known as corbelling. This is often used to support an oriel window or chimney stack.

examples of corbel-tables

cordon a type of circular stone moulding situated below the parapet of the REVETMENT (or retaining wall) of a fort.

cornice in the CLASSICAL ORDER, the structure at the top of the ENTABLATURE. Also, any ornamental moulding or projecting structure along the top of a wall, arch or exterior of a building.

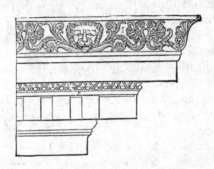

a Romanesque cornice

ornamental cornice

course a horizontal layer of stones, bricks or wood laid in a continuous row in a wall all at the same height. Coursed walling is a wall made of unworked stones placed in

courses. A lacing course is one which fixes the facing to
the main body of the wall. A string course is one which
projects out from the facing on the wall of a building and
is usually moulded.

coving a broad concave moulding, usually made of wood,
plaster or modern manufactured material, concealing and
ornamenting the junction between the walls and ceiling
of a room. Also, part of a ROOD SCREEN.

cowl a metal, revolving hood for a chimney which moves
with the wind for improved ventilation and escape of
smoke.

cross-domed church an early Christian or Byzantine
church, the plan of the main part being in the form of a
cross. There is a central domed roof while the four arms
of the cross are barrel-vaulted, supported by corner piers.
There are aisles and galleries of three sides and it may
also be called an ambulatory church.

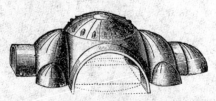

a cross-domed style Church

cross-in-square the most common plan for a Byzantine
church, also known as cross-inscribed with nine bays.
There is a large square central bay with a domed roof
resting on four COLUMNS or PIERS. The four corner bays are
small and square with domed or vaulted roofs. The other

four bays are rectangular in shape and usually barrel-vaulted.

crown the area of the upper surface of a VAULT, where the ribs intersect. The place of intersection is often covered by a BOSS and if a RIDGE RIB is present, it runs along the length of the crown of the vault.

cruck construction a form of building originating in Saxon times and continuing through the Middle Ages, using crucks (also called blades), which were enormous curved timbers extending from ground or near-ground level to meet at an apex above. Hence the crucks formed the framework for both the walls and roof. Early buildings were built in bays and were one storey high. There was a lack of headroom and the crucks themselves were curved tree trunks. Roofs were made of thatch, turf, brush or heather. The form of cruck construction underwent further modification as time went on, and eventually it became possible to erect large, two storey builidngs often for use as barns. Roofs were either thatched or tiled.

crypt a room, chamber or vault below floor level in a church, which may or may not be underground, usually used for burials or where relics are kept. A ring crypt is in the form of a half circle below the APSE of a church.

cupola a small domed roof on top of a turret which is usually circular or polygonal in plan.

curtain wall in a medieval castle, this is the outer wall which is fortified by BASTIONS or TOWERS along its length. Also, a type of wall which is not weight-bearing erected to protect a building from the effects of the weather.

culvert a drain constructed from stone or brick in the form of a tunnel which provides a channel for carrying water.

cusp a projecting point formed where two ornamental curved shapes meet as at the intersection of arcs or FOILS in GOTHIC TRACERY.

D

dado the solid block or cube which in classical architecture forms the body of a PEDESTAL between the plinth or base and the CORNICE above. Within a room it is part of the decorative scheme including the lower part of the wall upon which mouldings are arranged to resemble a pedestal. This usually comprises a skirting at the base and a moulding roughly at waist height, called the dado rail or CHAIR RAIL.

dado rail *see* **chair rail**

daïs a platform raised above floor level at the end of a hall. The term referred initially to the principal table or seat of honour at the table and the raised floor on which these were placed. In a medieval baronial hall the daïs would have extended across the whole of one end of the hall, often in front of a large window. The seats probably had a canopy over them, reflecting the word's origin from the old French for canopy.

diaper work (or diapering) a decoration, all over a surface, which consists of flowers in a square outline, diamonds or similar ornament. Carved flowers are usually sunk into the surface and it is found commonly in medieval gothic architecture. It was introduced in the Early English style (late 12th century) and continued into the Decorated style (end of the 13th century) and is to be found in, for example, Westminster Abbey.

diaphragm arch a transverse ARCH which forms a line

separating vaulting bays. It carries a masonry gable and provides a break between sections of timber roofs which act as a barrier to the spread of fire.

dipteral a PERISTYLE with a double COLONNADE.

dome a rounded roof, convex in shape, which covers part or all of a building. It is derived from the Italian *duomo* for cathedral because it was traditional to build a dome (or CUPOLA) over these buildings and the word became absorbed into general terminology. A dome is essentially a vault with a circular or near-circular base and sides of constant curvature. Its base on a flat plane can also be elliptical or polygonal and the dome itself may deviate from the spherical.

Domes are often constructed on a square base in which case a transitional structural element must be introduced to facilitate the meeting of square and circular features. This may be achieved through *pedentives* or *squinches*. A pedentive is a triangular section with a dome-like curvature which begins at a corner of the square as a pier and rises with increasing width to form a horizontal top which, with three other pedentives, forms the base upon which the dome can be accommodated. A squinch is a series of arches, each one above and projecting beyond the one beneath. If constructed from each corner of a square structure, the arches eventually meet to form a suitable base for the dome. Domes may also sit atop a circular base or drum.

The dome did not feature prominently until the Renaissance and Baroque styles and then it became a common design feature, utilising pedentives (a technique evolved in Byzantine architecture) to provide the necessary effects incorporating stone, light and decorative surfaces and features.

a dome illustrating pedantives

domical vault (also called a **cloister vault**) a vault shaped like a low DOME on a base which has a square or polygonal plan.

doors and **doorways** the means of entry into a room or building and which for its simple and fundamental function nevertheless has a varied and interesting history. Doors were made of metal or wood and initially very plain save for the iron hinges with scrollwork, nail heads and handles (as found with doors of the Norman style). This style continued for some time and in the 14th century decorative panels and ornamentation were introduced which became more complex in time. The classical door featured the use of panels, commonly six but ranging from two to ten, which were sunk and edged with moulding. Panelled doors attract a specific terminology of rails, panels and styles.

The doorway, which forms the framework into a building or room within which the door hangs, has evolved with the development of styles resulting in a multitude of forms. The Saxon doorway is typically plain and small with a semicircular arch and perhaps an IMPOST projecting from the face of the wall. Much more decoration and ornamentation was introduced in Romanesque doorways although this often featured only on the outside. The arch remained semi-circular but commonly was recessed deeply and moulded and because the door opening was often flat at the top, an intermediate semi-circular panel (TYMPANUM) afforded further opportunity for ornament and sculpture.

A pointed arch became the feature of doors from the Early English and Decorated periods. In addition there were numerous mouldings and the JAMBS consist of several small shafts and capitals and were generally carved with leaves or a similar decoration. The Decorated period mirrored those features although in a lighter style, and a particularly common ornament was the ball-flower and four-leaved flower.

a decorated Romanesque doorway

A noticeable change occurred in the Perpendicular period when a rectangular moulding contained the arch of the doorway and the SPANDRELS were ornamented in some way. Shafts commonly featured in the jambs although not as prominently as previously and the four-centred arch became a common feature. From the 1550s on, the doorway was rectangular with columns or PILASTERS and a PEDIMENT. Later, into the 18th century, a round arch enclosed the doorway, the LUNETTE above the door being formed into a decoration of glass or iron work in a fan shape.

a doorway in the pointed style at Cologne Cathedral

dormer window a window placed in a sloping roof. The window is vertical and by virtue of the resulting geometry, has its own roof and sides (or *cheeks*). Dormers allow access of light into an attic and in the past would have served as sleeping quarters, thus the name.

dosseret a feature found often in Byzantine architecture which comprises a four-faced IMPOST block or slab placed on top of an ABACUS before the arch above.

a typical Byzantine dosseret

double glazing windows with two layers of glass with an air space between. Such windows are commonly produced as sealed units within wood, aluminium or uPVC frames. The primary purpose of double glazing is for insulation (heat and also sound). Heat insulation reaches its maximum when the cavity is between 12 and 20mm, because larger gaps allow convection currents to become established thus increasing heat loss. Sound insulation is between 30 and 50 dB, over half as much again as single glazing.

dovetail a joint used to fasten together pieces of wood. The interlocking tenons (or pins) are shaped in the tail fan of a dove and because the ends are wider than the root, it makes a strong joint which cannot be easily pulled apart. It is used in the corners of drawers and fine joinery.

dowel commonly a short cylindrical rod of wood which is used to fasten together two pieces of wood. The two parts have predrilled holes to accommodate the dowel, the latter often being fluted to allow escape of air and glue as the joint is made. The dowel may also be made of metal, slate or similar material and be used to join or hold in place stone or concrete.

dressings stones that are worked to provide a finished face and which may be moulded or smooth and used around a window or as a feature. The dressings may form frames around openings in a brick building, i.e. around windows and doorways producing a more decorative and attractive appearance.

drip a projection, possibly in the form of a moulding or tablet, located above doorways, windows, arches and similar features. It is used to direct rainwater away from the wall below, although it is also found as an ornamental feature. The drip, or dripstone, may comprise a simple moulding with small ornaments (Norman) or in the case of Early English, terminate with a boss of foliage. The dripstone follows the general slope of the arch that it serves but in the Decorated period often takes the shape of an OGEE (*see also* HOOD-MOULD).

E

earth building a fairly crude method of construction using ADOBE, cob (clay soil with straw or roots) or pisé (dry loam with or without cement) and which is usually built by the occupier. The walls are thick, providing good insulation, but such constructions are very susceptible to earthquake damage and, unless protected, can be eroded by wind and rain. Earth buildings are appropriate for dry climates but material selection and construction must be correct to provide a safe dwelling.

eave the underneath part of a sloping roof that overhangs a wall.

efflorescence (also called bloom) the formation of powder-like crystals on the face of clay (but not calcium silicate) bricks. The white marks are unsightly, although not detrimental unless plaster or tiles are lifted as a result. The powder may be removed by brushing but plaster may require replacement.

egg and dart an OVOLO MOULDING that is decorated with egg shapes and arrow head, alternating along the moulding. It is frequently seen in classical architecture and may also be called the echinus, found beneath the ABACUS of a column.

Elizabethan architecture refers to the style of design and construction practised during the reign of Queen Elizabeth I (1558–1603). The style combined features of the

Renaissance (e.g. symmetry of façades) with the large windows of the Perpendicular and also aspects of Flemish architecture. There was a great deal of building during this period, directed primarily at the construction of large country houses (the *great* houses, such as Longleat House and Wollaton Hall) and the more traditional and smaller timber-framed houses (e.g Little Moreton Hall).

Elizabethan great houses retained a symmetry with an E or H shape in plan where the central bar formed the entrance and arranged symmetrically on either side were the windows, apartments and other features. Windows were commonly very large and dominated the walls, and gables became curved (the style seen in the Netherlands) and decorated. Ornamentation was also applied to chimney stacks.

The more simple wooden buildings displayed sloping gabled roofs and modest windows in walls comprising timber, brick and plaster. Wood panelling was a common internal feature as were plaster ceilings.

embrasure an opening in a wall, for a window or door, in which the sides are slanted from within. Also an opening in a parapet (also known as crenelle) which is also slanted on the inside.

enfilade the architectural design feature in which a series of internal doors to rooms were aligned so that a long view was obtained when all the doors were open. This was introduced in the 1650s and became a common feature in Baroque palaces. The term also applies to long rows of trees planted so as to create a similar long view or vista.

entablature the part of the structure, or order, which lies upon the columns. It consists of the lower ARCHITRAVE, followed by the frieze and the uppermost cornice. Each order has a typical entablature the height and subdivision of which relate to the column diameter.

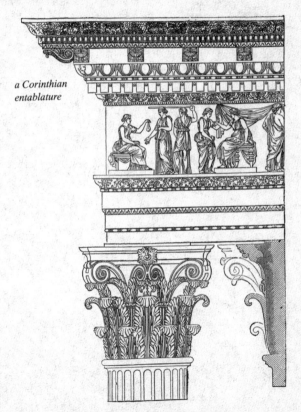

a Corinthian entablature

F

façade the front face of a building which may be in a particular architectural style not necessarily reflected in the rest.

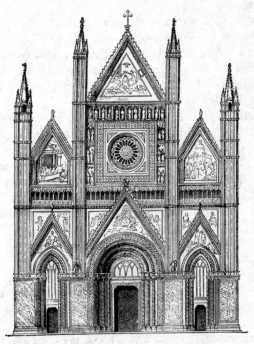

the façade of Orvieto Cathedral

facing the surface applied to the exterior of a building to finish it off which performs a protective and decorative function.

false ceiling a second ceiling constructed below the level of the original one, to reduce the height of a room usually for the purposes of warmth and insulation. It is usually supported on ceiling joists and often constructed out of plasterboard.

fanlight a window above a doorway, which was a common feature in 18th century houses, usually semicircular in shape with glazing bars radiating out from the centre resembling a lady's fan. The name was later applied to any window above a door or the upper portion of a hinged window.

fan vault a vault with panelling in the shape of a fan, having curving ribs of equal length arising from a single point or vaulting shaft at the top of the wall. As the ribs radiate outwards and upwards towards the CROWN of the vault, they are interrupted by semicircular LIERNE ribs running across them. The whole appearance of the vault is of a series of fans formed from inverted, concave cones.

fenestration the arrangement or plan of windows in a building.

fillet a raised block with a thin flat surface which runs vertically between the flutes on the shaft of a COLUMN or along circular moulding. Also, the upper part of a CORNICE.

finial an ornament which tops a PINNACLE, SPIRE, PEDIMENT, GABLE etc. often made of carved wood or stone in the form of a floral decoration or figure.

a tabernacle finial to a buttress   · *a finial in Cologne Cathedral*

fire resistance the degree to which a component of a building can resist the passing of a fire to another part, or can continue to support its load or perform its function.

flèche a very slender spire, also known as a spirelet, usually constructed of wood or metal and rising from the roof ridge. It normally occurs on a church roof taking the place of a tower at the point where two parts cross. The word flèche is French for arrow and this feature was common in France as it caused fewer structural problems, being much lighter.

fleur-de-lis, **fleur-de-lys** or **flower-de-luce** an ornament in the form of an heraldic lily flower used as a decoration in architecture.

a fleur-de-lis ornament

floor finishes material laid to form a finished surface on the sub-floor, e.g. floor coverings and modern flooring materials.

flush a flat surface which is level with any adjacent surface and all are on one plane.

flush bead moulding a rounded convex moulding which is sunk in so that its outer surface is level with the surface of the adjacent wall or door.

fluting shallow channels or grooves running vertically down the SHAFT of a COLUMN or other surface.

foil an ornamental feature especially of Gothic TRACERY meaning one small arc of a circle separated from adjacent ones by CUSPS. The number of foils in a design is named by giving it a prefix: *trefoil* (three), *quatrefoil* (four), *cinquefoil* (five), *multifoil* (many).

a trefoil and quatrefoil

folly an extravagant, useless construction usually erected in parkland by the wealthy owner of an estate. A folly was usually in the form of imitation classical or Gothic ruins, tower or fanciful structure of some kind.

formeret a non-structural rib in a VAULT BAY constructed along the side wall in order to complete a design. It is also known as a *wall rib*.

formwork any structure that contains and holds fresh, wet concrete in place until it sets. It may be constructed from wood, metal, fibreglass or other materials and includes other devices such as wedges, brackets and clips. Formwork is usually removed after twenty-four hours and leaves an impression of its structure on the surface of the concrete.

forum a feature of Roman cities which was an open space enclosed by colonnades and civic buildings.

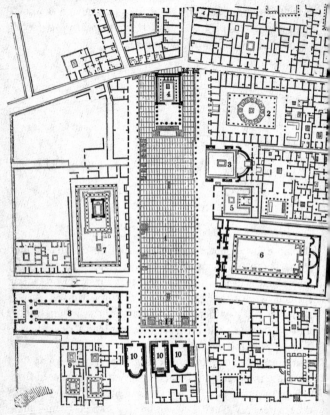

ground-plan of the Forum at Pompeii with the buildings surrounding it

1. the Forum. 2 the Pantheon. 3 Council hall of the Decurions. 4 Temple of Jupiter. 5 the so-called Temple of Quirinus. 6 Chalcidicum and Crypto-potico of Eumachia. 7 Temple of Venus. 8 Basilica. 9 Granaries. 10 the three Curiae. 11 School of Verna.

foundation the supporting solid ground beneath a building which carries and supports the overlying structure.

frame construction a building supported by a frame rather than weight-bearing walls as in TIMBER FRAMING and STEEL-FRAME CONSTRUCTION.

freestone a stone which is fine-grained, cuts easily and lacks bedding planes or laminations, e.g. oolitic limestones such as Portland stone, and some sandstones.

fret a type of ornament or decoration in the form of a geometrical design of repeated vertical and horizontal lines making a banded pattern.

examples of fret ornamentation

frieze the middle member of an ENTABLATURE between the CORNICE above and ARCHITRAVE below. Also, a broad decorative band below a CORNICE around the walls of a room, ornamented with painting or sculpture.

section of a Roman frieze

frontispiece the main entrance or **façade** of a building.

functionalism a theory or set of ideas, popular in the 1920s, which held that a building should first and foremost fulfil its function well and that artistic and aesthetic considerations should be of secondary importance.

G

gable the upper triangular part (above the eaves) of the end wall of a building which rises to a point in the middle to match the roof pitch. The sides are normally straight but can be curved or stepped, the latter predating the former. Shaped gables are characteristic of the 1600s. A Dutch gable features a pediment on top of the gable. Gable end is the term given to the wall containing the gable.

gable of house in Germany during the Rococo period of the Renaissance

galilee a porch, vestibule or chapel at the west end of a church which was considered less sacred than the remainder of the building. The galilee was used by penitents or women in the early Middle Ages and there was some line of division, perhaps an architectural feature, to signify its difference from the rest of the church. Galilees were incorporated into Lincoln, Ely and Durham cathedrals.

gallery a structural feature found in many different buildings and performing a number of functions. In churches, the gallery is a long, narrow upper storey which opens on to the body of the church, often on to the nave. It may hold the organ loft and choir. A gallery may also be an exterior feature and is found in medieval churches in Italy and Germany.

At the opposite end to the DAÏS in medieval halls was often constructed a minstrels' gallery and in theatres the gallery refers to the upper tiers of seats. In many cases, the gallery is supported on columns or CORBELS. In the 16th and 17th centuries long galleries in England often extended the full length of a house on the second floor. Such rooms were used for entertainment or recreation and in time paintings were often hung in the gallery, leading ultimately to the term, art gallery.

galleting the primarily decorative technique of pushing pebbles or chips of stone into mortar which is still soft.

garderobe the term for a wardrobe in medieval houses and castles in which clothes or items of value would be stored. The garderobe would often be constructed within the outer stone wall. Also the medieval term for a lavatory.

gargoyle a spout projecting from a roof or parapet used especially in Gothic architecture to throw water from the gutter away from the walls. Gargoyles may be plain but are often carved into human or animal forms and commonly present grotesque faces. The mouth tends to be open allowing an escape of water, but water spouts may be incorporated above or below the stone. The Early

English style was when gargoyles first appeared at which time they were quite prominent. The usual site for gargoyles is in the CORNICE but sometimes they occur on the front face of a buttress.

gargoyles at Cologne Cathedral

gatehouse the entrance gateway to a building, town or city which also housed the person responsible for checking those people entering and leaving. In the Middle Ages and before, structures such as castles, abbeys, large houses and also towns had protective walls with gatehouses. A fine example can be seen today in York at the Middlegate Bar, which dates from the early 13th century. Gatehouses often formed large impressive constructions and in military buildings there might be a portcullis at either end. The ceiling would be vaulted and perforated with holes sufficiently large to enable missiles to be thrown on anyone below in the event of a battle. The gatehouse is usually rectangular in plan with towers at front and rear containing stairs to upper chambers.

Gatehouses became more decorative in the 15th and early 16th centuries as their military use declined and Tudor versions were often quite ornate and constructed of brick or stone.

gazebo a summerhouse or small pavilion within a garden or park and commanding a fine view. Occasionally these are seen on the roof of a house (*see* BELVEDERE).

geodesic dome a structure developed by Buckminster Fuller in which a hemisphere is created by joining light rods in hexagonal shapes. This is a type of *space frame* which enables a construction to span a large area with few or no supporting structures.

Georgian architecture refers to architecture during the period 1714 to 1830, the reigns of four King Georges. The style is essentially classical in design and interiors tend to be more elaborate than exteriors. Many well-known architects practised during this period, notably Robert Adam who was renowned for his decorative style.

Many Country houses were built during this period and the dominant style in the first half of the 18th century was PALLADIAN. The latter half of this century saw greater diversification and interior design became detailed and grand producing elegant buildings with excellent craftsmanship.

Gibbs surround the extremity of a window or doorway which contains blocks of stone set around the frame. The blocks alternate between large and small and a keystone arrangement usually features at the head of the opening.

glass the use of glass, initially to create decorative objects or glaze-like coatings, and then to form vessels before its widespread use in architecture, has a long history and probably began about six thousand years ago. Its use was purely decorative until the late 18th century when it was used in greenhouses and similar structures. Before this time its primary functional use was in windows but it was only found in the homes of privileged people until well into the 15th century. With time, glass became more common in domestic architecture, although initially a protective wooden lattice was fitted because the glass was valuable.

Eventually glass was used for the construction of complete buildings, e.g. Crystal Palace in 1851, and also for large span roofs as seen in large railway stations (e.g. Paddington) and stores. Subsequently it achieved the universal usage of today whereby glass is used extensively including whole building façades.

Over the years the technology of glass production has changed dramatically. Up until the 1700s, it was produced as cylinder glass in which a hollow cylinder was blown, cut open and then flattened. At this time the demand for glass increased and the use of wood for fuel was banned so coal was used to fire the furnaces. Crown glass reappeared in the late 1700s, although it had earlier been produced in the 16th century. This glass was manufactured as a disc of varying sizes, thicker in the middle, and being of better quality was admirably suited to Georgian windows.

Plate glass was introduced in the early 17th century although production was adopted only slowly in Britain, due to the high cost of establishing a factory. Plate glass could be made thicker than crown glass and polished to a near perfect finish but, because it was expensive, it found use primarily as mirrors initially. As demand rose in the late 18th century, the first factory was built in England and eventually, in the latter part of the 19th century, plate glass was used in large panes for department stores, factories and large houses. Sheet glass which used a similar technique to cylinder glass but enabled larger panes to be made, was employed in the Crystal Palace.

Developments continued apace into the 20th century, including rolled plate glass where glass in molten form is fed between rollers cooled by water. Perhaps the most remarkable development in glass production came in the 1950s when float glass was developed, based upon the idea proposed by Sir Alastair Pilkington. Essentially, molten glass is floated onto a bed of molten tin which allows glass of high quality and clarity to be produced.

There are numerous speciality glasses, including laminated (safety) glass which is a sandwich of plastic in glass and other safety glasses such as wired glass. Stained glass is a special type of glass that has a long history, originating probably in ancient Egypt. Church and cathedral windows of the Middle Ages used stained glass extensively and colours were obtained by several methods: mixing oxides of metals with the glass; burning a pigment onto the surface, or flashing which involved a double-layered piece of glass being blown, white on one side and coloured on the other. Inevitably technology advanced and styles changed over the centuries, but stained glass remains an important decorative technique particularly in religious buildings. In modern architecture glass is also used in a variety of products, such as slabs, bricks and tubing.

Gothic architecture an architectural style found in Europe between the late 1100s and the mid 1500s. It is typified by a number of features including pointed arches, flying buttresses, the rib vault, tracery on windows, a minimising of walls by incorporation of arcades or galleries, slender pier and a tendency to vertical features such as steeples. These are not specifically Gothic features, but appeared elsewhere at different times. However, the Gothic style brought them all together in a unified theme and it was seen particularly in the impressive medieval cathedrals which employed spires, arches and buttresses to the full, creating upward-reaching designs.

The Gothic style evolved from Romanesque and there were four identifiable periods between 1066 and the 1550s, namely Norman, Early English, Decorated and Perpendicular. Over the years, walls became thinner and had supporting buttresses, buildings were larger and higher and overall wall area was reduced by the incorporation of large windows and doorways. Inevitably, design and construction practice advanced to accommodate and facilitate the architectural developments and allowed the use of pillars and ribs, vaults and abutments. The complex design then gave rise to the immense, yet ornate structures of this style.

The four styles of Gothic are not rigid divisions and there is overlap and transition between them, and considerable differences in the chronology between different areas.

The Early English or First Pointed style is characterized by a simple approach with plain ribbed vaults, windows without tracery and tall piers with shafts grouped together. An excellent example is Salisbury Cathedral. The

Decorated phase (or Middle Pointed) followed and lasted
for about 100 years, until the mid 1370s. It shows the flying buttresses and large windows with decorative heads,
fan vaults, smaller wall areas and greater ornamentation

House at Greifswald

on the stone and in the use of window glass. The next phase, Perpendicular, lasted a long time but changed little, employing vertical lines and features with towers, ornamented flying buttresses, large windows with tracery

Rheims Cathedral

and a maximum use of doorways and windows. A typical example is the Henry VII Chapel in Westminster Abbey. Tudor Gothic followed the Perpendicular, and boasts much fine architecture, e.g. Trinity College Chapel in Cambridge.

Lichfield Cathedral

Even after the end of the Gothic architectural period, the style recurred, albeit in modified form and at the whim of individual architects. The Gothic Revival proper occurred around the middle of the 19th century and included the Palace of Westminster which was rebuilt after the fire of 1834. In Britain the Revival was at its peak between 1855 and 1885 and it was applied to a whole range of buildings, from town halls to railway stations.

the Houses of Parliament in the late 19th century

groin the angle or edge created where two or more vaults intersect.

groined vault this is also known as a *cross vault* because it is formed from two identical BARREL VAULTS which meet at right angles.

grotesque a type of ornamentation/decoration employing paintings, carvings or stucco, depicting human and animal forms often in a mythical representation, with associated floral motifs. Also known as arabesque, it derives from grotto, the Italian for a subterranean apartment, because the original Roman forms were discovered buried in ruins during the Renaissance.

typical grotesque sculpture on a capital

grotto an artificial cave or cavern, originally a Roman feature but revived during the Renaissance. Grottoes were decorated with sculpture, ceramics and invariably included fountains and water cascading over rock and shell formations. Some large houses of the 17th and 18th centuries contained grottoes.

guilloche a decorative pattern used on mouldings which consists of a plait of interlaced bands.

a guilloche pattern

H

herringbone a zigzag pattern of bricks, tiles or stones achieved by laying alternate courses in diagonal lines in opposite directions, instead of horizontally. This produces a decorative fish backbone pattern in a wall.

high-rise building up until the 1880s, it was not possible to erect buildings beyond twelve storeys high because the walls would have been enormously thick at the base in order to bear the load. There was a great desire to erect tall buildings especially in American cities where land prices were very high. During the 1880s, the idea of using a metal framework to bear the weight of the building was developed, and "skyscrapers" started to become a reality. In the early years of high rise building, features of classical or Gothic architecture were often incorporated. In the 1920s and 30s skyscrapers rose higher than ever before, particularly in America, e.g. the Empire State Building, and designs became plainer. Since the Second World War, high-rise buildings have been erected in most countries and advances in technology have eased the problems of construction (*see* REINFORCED CONCRETE). However, the use of this type of building for homes, in the form of blocks of flats, is now unpopular in Britain due to the social problems which have occurred.

hip the angle formed on the outside at the junction of two sloping roof surfaces.

hood mould or **dripstone** a moulding which projects out from the face of a wall above a doorway, window or arch to divert rainwater. If the moulding is rectangular in shape, it is called a label and an ornamental carving at the end is known as a label stop.

an example of a hood mould over a window

hypaethral lacking a roof and open to the sky.

hyperbolic parabloid roof a type of roof with a double curve formed from a rectangular shape folded across the diagonal. The geometric shape is made by straight lines running in a continuous plane from one parabolic arch to another, and is relatively simple to construct.

hypocaust a chamber beneath the floor of a Roman building which was part of the central heating system and constructed of stone or brick. Hot air and gases generated by a furnace heated the chamber and hence the rooms above. These then escaped through flues built into the walls heating other rooms in the process.

hypogeum a vault or chamber built underground.

hypostyle a large space which may be a room or hall in which the roof is supported on numerous columns.

I

insulation any one of a number of materials used in buildings to prevent heat loss. There are two main types, cellular and reflective insulation. Cellular, in the form of expanded foam is made into boards, loose fill, flock or moulded insulation. Reflective insulation is in the form of special paints or coatings or aluminium foil for radiators. Cellular insulation may be installed in the roof space, walls or under a ground floor. Double glazing of windows provides both thermal and sound insulation.

intrados also called a soffit, this is the curve on the underside of an ARCH.

ionic *see* **classical order**

ironwork iron was in use for centuries as a tough and hard-wearing material for the manufacture of weapons and agricultural implements. The type of metal used was wrought iron which was hammered and beaten into the correct shape. In the Middle Ages, the development of tall blast furnaces using wood as fuel made it possible to produce cast iron implements and weapons. The decline of forests and availability of wood for fuel, meant that coal had to be used for the smelting of iron. The results remained unsatisfactory, producing brittle iron which was too weak to be of much use until the process of coking the coal was developed in the early 1700s. Later the development of the steam engine, and stirring or puddling the molten iron to remove impurities, paved the way for the widespread use of the metal in many aspects of construction. From the 1780s through to the 1900s, iron was used extensively in the construction of bridges and buildings. It was especially popular for support and reinforcement of masonry and timber, door and window frames, BALUSTRADES, BALCONIES, railings, COLUMNS and BEAMS. Both wrought and cast iron was used both for constructional and ornamental features. Decorative ironwork was especially popular in staircase BALUSTRADES, BALCONIES and railings. Iron reinforcement, COLUMNS and BEAMS were used in many buildings such as textile mills, factories, public buildings, churches and halls. The 984 feet high Eiffel Tower in Paris, made from wrought iron, is just one of many fine examples of the use of ironwork.

isometric projection a method of geometrical drawing to produce a plan of a building in three dimensions. Vertical lines remain vertical while other lines are drawn at an equal angle, which is usually 30º, to the horizontal. The plan gives an illusion of normal perspective because the dimensions are drawn correctly to scale. In an *axonometric projection,* a three-dimension plan of a building is drawn at a chosen angle. The horizontal and vertical lines are drawn to scale but there is distortion of curves and diagonals.

J

Jacobean architecture the style of building and decoration which occurred during the reign of James I of England (1603–25). On the whole this was a continuation of the architectural style of the Elizabethan period but on a grander and more lavish scale. Few church buildings were constructed during this period so the style is reflected mainly in large mansion houses such as Blickling Hall, Norfolk. The plan of the building was usually in the form of an H or E and rooms were designed in Classical style, with an interpretation of the Classical order. There was a great staircase of carved oak, a very prominent feature which ascended around an open well. The long gallery was another characteristic feature of a Jacobean mansion with very highly decorated wood and plasterwork. Also, ceilings were very richly and beautifully decorated in plasterwork. Jacobean architects were influenced by Flemish rather than Italian forms and surviving mansions include Aston Hall, Birmingham and Hatfield House, Hertfordshire.

jamb the vertical side supports of a doorway, arch, window or fireplace.

jetty the projection outwards of an upper storey of a building beyond the dimensions of the storey below, in a timber-framed building. The beams and joists above the lower storey project beyond the external wall and carry the walling for the storey above on their outer ends.

Buildings which are jettied often have a dragon beam (*see* BEAM) running diagonally and carrying the JOISTS.

jib door also known as a *gib door*, this is a concealed door hidden in the surface of a wall. It is flush with the surrounding wall surface and decorated in an identical manner with no interruption in the mouldings or other ornamentation.

joggle, joggling terminology used by masons for interlocking two blocks or stones together, so that they do not move or slip by means of a projecting peg in one and groove or notch in the other. This can often be seen in the surface of an ARCH, but if hidden, it is called a *secret joggle*.

joist one of a series of parallel beams laid horizontally which support the floorboards of a roof above. Often, ceiling laths are fastened to the undersurface of the beams for the support of a plaster ceiling for the room below.

K

keel moulding a type of curved moulding which is reminiscent of the keel of a ship in profile.

keep *see* **castle**

Kentish rag a type of hard, weather-resistant limestone found in Kent and widely used as building stone.

keystone *see* **arch**

kiosk a feature of Persian and Turkish architecture, a SUMMERHOUSE or PAVILION which is an airy structure supported by pillars. In Britain and Europe, they were adapted as, for example, bandstands in public parks or, in modern times, as small shops selling ice cream, confectionery, etc.

kit house a type of INDUSTRIALIZED BUILDING which is usually a timber-framed house made up of prefabricated parts. The name may apply to the framework alone but can include the whole house with all its finishings.

knapped flint flints which are laid in the surface of a wall. The flints are split in two and laid so that the shiny black surfaces show in the face of the wall. This is a common feature in East Anglia.

L

laced windows a type of decorative feature in which the vertical lines formed by the sides of a window are continued upwards and downwards, usually in brickwork of a different colour to that of the surrounding wall. This has the effect of joining together the windows above and below and was popular in the 1720s in England.

lacunar a word which applies to both the panels of a COFFERED ceiling and the whole panelled or coffered ceiling itself.

lancet windows a very narrow, arched and pointed window common to fortified buildings in the early 1200s.

lantern a small turret, polygonal or circular in plan, occurring on the top of a roof or dome to let in air and light.

lattice window a window with diagonal glazing bars in which are set rectangular or diamond-shaped LEADED LIGHTS.

leaded lights the diamond-shaped or rectangular panes of glass which occur in a LATTICE WINDOW.

leaf-and-dart a type of OVOLO moulding, especially used under the cushion of CAPITALS in the IONIC order (*see* CLASSICAL ORDER). It consists of alternating leaf and dart shapes.

lierne an extra, non-structural rib in a vaulted roof, numbers of which may be present crossing other ribs to make an elaborate pattern.

lierne vault a ribbed VAULT with extra ribs called LIERNE.

lights the openings between the upright posts or MULLIONS of a window.

lightweight concrete concrete weighing less than 1900kg/m^3 of which there are two types. Aerated concrete is made from cellular material which is highly insulating although not very strong. It weighs up to 800kg/m^3 and is used as a casing for columns or steel beams. Lightweight aggregate is used to make concrete which is less dense than normal concrete but with better insulating properties, and can be used for structural components such as beams, blocks and columns.

lintel a horizontal beam of wood or stone lying over an opening such as a doorway, and supporting the wall above.

loggia a room, gallery or arcade open on one or more sides which is often supported by a colonnade.

longhouse a type of Viking dwellinghouse introduced into Britain by the Norse invaders. It was a long, low type of house and dwellings of this kind were being built in stone by 800 AD in Orkney, Shetland and the north of Scotland by descendants of the Vikings. Turf was rammed into the gaps between the stones and a timber frame supported a thatch, heather or turf roof weighted down with stones.

louvre an opening in the roof of a medieval hall or kitchen to allow for the escape of steam and smoke from a fire in the hearth below. The opening was often surrounded by a TURRET or LANTERN with slanting boards which diverted rainwater. Later, the term louvre was applied to one of a number of overlapping, slanting boards or panes of glass. (Also, *lever* and *luffler*).

lucarne either a small opening or window in a spire or attic or a DORMER window.

lunette an opening, panel or window, in the shape of a half-circle often found above a door (*see* FANLIGHT).

lych gate derived from the Saxon word *lych* meaning corpse, the lych gate was a covered wooden entrance or gateway to a churchyard where a coffin could be rested before proceeding.

M

machicolation a defensive structure in the form of a projecting PARAPET on an outside wall of a castle, supported on CORBELS or BRACKETS. There were openings in the floor of the parapet through which missiles and boiling oil could be launched at attackers besieging the castle.

mannerism a term applied in two ways in architecture. Firstly, it is applied to a rigid, strict form of classicism but, more commonly, to the use of classical ornament and decoration in a way which departs from the norm. In Italy during the 16th century, some of the great architects and artists such as Michelangelo deliberately broke away from the accepted classical rules to create new effects. In Britain, especially in ELIZABETHAN and JACOBEAN domestic architecture, the classical rules were accidentally broken because they were not well understood.

manor house a country house belonging to the lord of the manor—the principal mansion house in a village or estate. Architecturally, it refers to an unfortified country mansion house of the late Middle Ages. At this time, there was little or no need for fortification, and the gatehouse (the upper storey of which was often used as a chapel) was more decorative than defensive. The house itself was built around a courtyard and was up to three STOREYS high with roofs at different levels. The hall extended through two storeys and was a prominent feature and reception rooms and bedrooms were laid out with more attention to comfort than had been the case in the past. An example of a fine manor house of this period is that at Great Chalfield (Wiltshire).

mansard roof *see* **roof**

mantelpiece also called a *chimney piece* (*see* CHIMNEY), this is the surrounding structure of a fireplace made of wood, stone, marble or brick. It often includes an overlying mirror or over-mantle above.

Martello tower a type of low, round tower built for defensive purposes with a flat roof on which guns were mounted. They were constructed for coastal defence, especially during the Napoleonic wars but were also used more widely and in many different countries.

masonry the craft carried out by masons of building with stone. In earlier times, pieces of rough stone or blocks which had been crudely shaped were usually held together with some form of MORTAR. However, building without mortar had also been carried out since very ancient times and this is known as *dry stone walling*. The ancient Mycenaean people used massive heavy stones which stayed in place because of their weight. Any gaps were filled with smaller stones rammed into position and this type of construction is termed *cyclopean*. Most early stone buildings in Britain and Europe had walls of *rubble construction*. Cut stone was so expensive that it was reserved for the facings of only the most important buildings. Rubble walls were constructed of small rough stones which were either laid randomly but sometimes were arranged in courses, and held with mortar. In later centuries, cut and dressed stone came to be more widely used even for more modest sized buildings. The stonework of the finest quality was known as ASHLAR.

mausoleum a grand construction built as a monument to contain a tomb. The name is derived from the monument built for King Mausolus who died in 353 BC, ordered by Queen Artemisia. This is known as the Mausoleum of Halicarnassus in modern Bodrum.

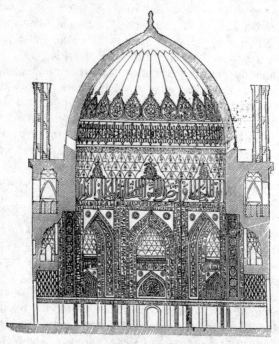

section of the mausoleum at Sultanieh

merlon a raised portion in a BATTLEMENT.

mews a line of stables built at the back of a town house, particularly in London, constructed with living accommodation above to house the groom or coachman. These are now converted into mews flats or houses.

mezzanine also called an *entresol*, this is a lower STOREY flanked by two higher ones.

minaret a structure of Eastern architecture connected with the Islamic faith. It is a tall, slender turret or tower which may be round, pencil-shaped or rectangular with one or more BALCO-NIES projecting outwards from its walls. The balcony is used by the *Muezzin* who uses it as a platform from which to summon the people to prayer in the MOSQUE.

an Egyptian minaret

minster originally this was the name given to any monastic community or its church. Later, the term came to be applied to some important churches and cathedrals such as York Minster.

Modern architecture the name given to the architectural style which has gradually developed in many countries since the First World War. It was prompted by three factors. Firstly, pressure from an expanding population in many cities which began during the 1800s. Secondly, a desire for change and a break from the traditions of the past with a view to constructing buildings in an *international style*, fulfilling the needs of 20th century peoples in many different countries. Thirdly, the need to build quickly following the destruction caused by two world wars, especially the Second World War.

Germany had a wealth of talented architects in the 1920s and 30s, many of whom became refugees. Some other European architects also were forced to become refugees and many eventually settled in America, sometimes after a period of time in Britain. Architecture in Britain at that time was dominated by those of a traditionalist frame of mind. However, under the influence of the continental refugees, some young British architects became more interested in modern architecture and broke away from the established traditional school. Once the Second World War was over, modern architecture became widely accepted as the way forward. Buildings relying on steel, glass, concrete and modern materials were extensively constructed in many countries throughout the world. There is now a great reliance on INDUSTRIALIZED BUILDING techniques and less reliance than at any time in the past on the traditional skills of masons and craftsmen.

modular design modules are units of measurement used to determine the proportions of a building. Hence, modular design is based on MODULES producing buildings of fixed proportions usually using pre-fabricated parts.

module a unit of measurement which regulates the proportions of a building. In CLASSICAL ARCHITECTURE the measurement used was the diameter or half the diameter of a COLUMN divided into sixty minutes. In modern architecture the module has become very important in the standardization of building parts.

modulor a system of measurement devised by the Swiss architect Le Corbusier, based upon the proportions of the parts of the male body. He named this system *Le Modulor*.

monastery *see* **abbey**

monolith a single, often massive, block of stone erected as a monument or column, sometimes singly or as one of a group.

monopteral a TEMPLE which lacks walls, the roof of which is supported by a series of COLUMNS.

mortar a mixture of sand, cement and water applied wet between stones, bricks or rubble in a wall to bind them together.

mortice and tenon a type of joint for fixing together two beams or shaped lengths of wood. The *tenon* is a projecting piece of peg from one beam which fits into a slot or socket called the *mortice* (mortise) in the other.

mosaic a type of decoration on the surface of walls or floors consisting of numerous small shaped and coloured pieces of glass, pottery, stone or marble, set in mortar or cement. Mosaics depicted both artistic scenes and geometrical patterns and were especially popular as decoration in Roman and Byzantine architecture.

a geometric mosaic

mosque an Islamic religious building constructed for prayer and worship, originally based on the plan of the house of the prophet Mohammed. Eventually, most mosques were constructed with at least one MINARET.

façade of the Sultan Ahmed Mosque at Constantinople

interior view of the mosque at Cordova

motte-and-bailey *see* **castle**

mouldings moulded or worked surfaces given to projecting parts or edges of a building. Many are ornamental features but others have a protective function. In CLASSICAL

ARCHITECTURE mouldings are used in specific and definite ways, often with their own particular type of ornamentation, and are often characteristic of their Order and period of architecture.

profiles of various mouldings

mullion an upright or vertical dividing bar in a window separating it into two LIGHTS.

mutule a square projecting block of stone under the soffit of the CORNICE of a Greek Doric ENTABLATURE. One mutule is set over each TRIGLYPH (*see* CLASSICAL ORDER).

N

naos the sanctuary chamber of a Greek temple which contained the statue of the god. Also, the sanctuary of a Byzantine church.

nave the western arm of a church which is west of the crossing. It usually refers to the middle part of the western arm where the congregation gathers and which is flanked by AISLES.

the nave of a Romanesque church

necking a type of narrow convex moulding situated at the base of a CAPITAL between it and the shaft of a COLUMN.

necropolis a graveyard or burial ground normally situated in or near a city.

niche a small recess usually concave and arched, which is set into a wall or other structure and generally contains a statue or other ornament.

nogging the filling in of the spaces between the timbers in a TIMBER-FRAMED building, usually with bricks to form a pattern, this being known as *brick nogging*.

nosing this is usually applied to the rounded edge of a stair but also to any such edge on a projecting moulding.

O

obelisk a type of stone MONOLITH which is tall and needle-like and tapers at one end. They were a feature of ancient Egyptian civilization and an example is Cleopatra's needle in London.

oculus a circular opening in the top of a roof dome or in a wall.

odeon a word derived from the Greek *odeion* or the Latin *odeum* meaning a small, roofed classical theatre.

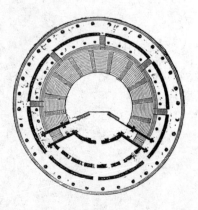

an odeon at Athens

off-set a sloping or horizontal surface in the face of a wall which is caused by a reduction in thickness in the

140

upper part. The lower part of the wall is thicker than the upper part and this creates the off-set surface, and there may be a projecting moulding on the outer edge to allow for the run-off of rainwater. A buttress off-set or *set-off* in a medieval castle has a sloping surface.

ogee a line with a double curve formed by a concave and convex portion as in an S or backward S. An ogee moulding has a double curved profile which is convex below and concave above, also called *Cyma recta*. A *reverse ogee moulding* is concave below and convex above and is also called *Cyma reversa*.

an ogee moulding

ogive a name applied in French architecture to describe a pointed ARCH.

opisthodomus the small room found at the back of the NAOS in a Greek TEMPLE which was usually used as a treasury.

opus incertum a type of Roman walling which is of random RUBBLE construction.

opus listatum a type of Roman walling in which courses of brick and small stone blocks alternate with one another.

opus quadratum a type of Roman walling using shaped squared stones.

opus reticulatum a type of Roman walling using worked squared stones which are arranged diagonally to form a diamond-shaped mesh pattern.

an example of opus reticulatum

ormolu a type of gold-coloured gilding which was extensively used for the decoration of fireplaces, doors, furniture and marble and stone surfaces, especially during the 18th century.

orchestra a feature of the Classical Greek theatre which was a central circular space, the *dancing floor*. In a Roman theatre, the corresponding part is called the *proscenium* and is in the shape of a half-circle.

oubliette a concealed and secret prison cell or dungeon in a medieval castle, the access being a trapdoor through which the prisoner was dropped.

overhang also known as an *oversail,* a part of a building or upper storey which projects outwards over a lower part.

ovolo moulding a rounded convex moulding, usually a quarter of a circle (*quarter-round*) in profile, which often has EGG AND DART ornamentation in classical buildings.

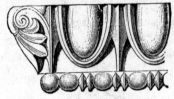

typical ovolo moulding

P

pagoda a European name describing a Japanese or Chinese Buddhist temple. Most are buildings of several storeys in tiered form with an irregular outline. They are called *shoro* or *tahoto* in Japan, *ta* in China and *stupas* in Burma.

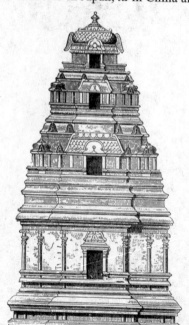

a Chinese pagoda

Palladian architecture a style of architecture which was based on, and evolved from, the work of a great 16th century Italian architect, Andrea Palladio (1508–80). Palladio was one of the first true architects of importance, as he studied and trained in this discipline alone whereas his predecessors considered themselves to be masters of several art forms. Palladio, in common with other architects of his time, derived his ideas from the classical architecture of ancient Rome, studying the works of VITRUVIUS and making many detailed drawings of buildings. He drew together various Renaissance ideas, particularly combining those of the symmetry of Roman town planning with the theory of *harmonic proportions*, relating architecture to music. Hence he was influenced by different sources and architects, the MANNERISM of Vignola and Michelangelo, the classical ideas of Bramante, the Byzantine architecture of Venice and concepts derived from his own studies. He built many palaces, villas, churches and public buildings and, in essence, adapted Roman ideas to the requirements of 16th century peoples by combining and altering various features. Most of his buildings were in Venice and Vicenza, notably his version of the Basilica in Vicenza. Palladio's designs for villas and churches were based on the Roman temple plan. One of the most important villas was the Villa Capra near Vicenza, versions of which were later copied in other countries.

The first English architect to be strongly influenced by the work of Palladio was Inigo Jones (1573–1652). His ideas were also highly influential in Holland from the 1650s onwards. However, both Dutch and English architects brought their own ideas and interpretations to bear on Palladianism in an individual way. There was a great revival of Palladianism in England, particularly in the building of mansions and country houses in the years 1720 to 1760 under the influence of Colen Campbell and Lord Burlington. Also around this time, the ideas of Palladianism were influential in several other countries including Germany, Russia and America.

the palace at Vicenza, by Palladio

palmette a type of classical decorative motif which is fan-shaped and may resemble a palm leaf or honeysuckle flowers. Palmette decorative forms were widely used by Renaissance architects and also later during the latter part of the 18th century.

palmette decoration

panel and panelling a panel is one of a number of flat wooden boards used to line the interior walls of a room. From the 13th century it became the usual practice to line interior walls with overlapping wooden boards which were held together with tongue and groove, and this was known as WAINSCOTING. WAINSCOT was later used to describe the type of wood used which was normally oak imported from Holland, Germany and Russia. In the 15th century, true wood panelling, using frame and panel construction, was introduced into Britain from Flanders and remained popular for hundreds of years. The thinner panels were set into grooves in a framework of thicker horizontal pieces, called *rails*, and vertical ones known as *stiles*. The pieces of the framework were themselves joined together by MORTICE AND TENON joints. This type of panelling was used, not only for the lining of walls, but also for ceilings, furniture and doors. Early panelling tended to be painted rather than carved, but in later years carving became much more common and different types of decoration were characteristic of a particular period. A type known as *linenfold* was popular from 1490–1550 (probably called *lignum undulatum* at the time), which represented a piece of highly folded material with the folds running vertically. A later refinement was the introduction of an *embroidered border* around the panel using a series of punched holes.a Greater variation was introduced during the 1500s and from 1630 onwards, the whole room was designed as classical order. Inlay, gilt and paint were used as ornamentation. Later, panels became plainer once again but were often sunk or sometimes raised in the centre (called *fielded*). In the 18th century, pine and deal wood were used instead of oak and sometimes these were painted.

pantile a roof tile which is s-shaped in profile.

parapet a low wall constructed along the edge of any structure where there is a sudden drop such as a balcony, roof top or on a bridge. A parapet may be in the form of a BATTLEMENT or decorated in some way.

parclose a screen in a church which divides a shrine or chapel from the main area of the building.

pargeting in early Medieval times, this was the name given to any type of coarse PLASTER work applied to the outside walls of a building. Pargeting, also known as *parge work*, *pargetry*, or *pargetting*, is now used to describe the decorative panels of plasterwork on the external walls of a TIMBER-FRAMED building. This was popular from Elizabethan times onwards, but its use declined as fewer timber-framed buildings were constructed in later centuries. The earliest examples which survive today date from the 1650s. Patterns were simple at first and named after the tool used to make them, e.g. *stick work* and *comb work*. Later, designs became more elaborate using animal, floral, heraldic and geometric patterns. When the plasterwork became dirty it was washed with lime or even coloured, and this eventually tended to obscure the design. If the process was carried out too often, the extra weight of the layers of paint caused the panels to break away so that the plaster needed to be renewed.

parquet, parquetry thin, polished strips of wood laid, usually in a herringbone pattern, as a floor covering fastened onto a wooden sub-surface. Strips of different colours are used to produce a polished floor which is always laid in a geometrical pattern.

patio a feature of Spanish architecture which spread to South America, being a type of central courtyard open to the sky.

pavilion a word that is used to describe a variety of features. Firstly, a pavilion may be a part of a building that projects out from the main block, usually in the centre or at the ends. It is usually square in plan and often has a domed roof. Secondly, it may be the end structure of a side wing, again often with a domed roof. Thirdly, a separate building of light and airy construction often ornamental, in a sports ground or park used for recreational purposes.

examples of Chinese pavilions

the pavilion of a Chinese temple

pedenture *see* **dome**.

pedestal a supporting structure beneath a column, statue or ornament such as an urn. In CLASSICAL ARCHITECTURE, the pedestal has three parts, the PLINTH at the base, DADO in the middle and CORNICE at the top.

pediment in CLASSICAL ARCHITECTURE, a low-pitched triangular-shaped GABLE surmounting the ENTABLATURE, formed by the incline of two sides of a sloping CORNICE which meet at an apex at the top. Pediments were similarly used as decorative features especially above doors, windows and recesses etc. A *broken* pediment is one in which the base moulding is interrupted by a gap, usually in the centre. An *open* pediment is one lacking the apex of the triangle. In a *segmental* pediment the upper part is curved rather than triangular in shape.

pele tower also known as a peel tower, this was a type of small defensive building constructed in the border regions of England and Scotland. Cattle were kept in the lower storey while people lived on the floor above, access being by means of a ladder or other types of steps which could be pulled up into the building.

pendant a projection from a ceiling BOSS which hangs downwards into a room. It was a feature of late Gothic architecture and also of vaulted and stucco ceilings in the 16th and early 17th centuries in England and France.

penthouse usually a structure with a separate roof at the top of a high building.

pergola a covered walkway in a garden formed from two rows of upright pillars supporting horizontal beams above which there is a profusion of climbing plants.

peripteral a temple surrounded by a single row of free-standing COLUMNS (*see* PERISTYLE).

peristyle a series of COLUMNS surrounding a court, TEMPLE or CLOISTER, other building or open space.

perron a platform on the outside of a building, reached by a flight of steps, which is usually the access to a first floor entrance.

pew a fixed seat made of wood in a church. In medieval churches, the end of the pew opening into the AISLE was usually finished with a *bench-end*. This often had a FINIAL at the top known as a POPPY HEAD which was carved ornamentally with flowers or figures of animals or humans. Another type of pew of a later date was the *box pew*. This was an enclosed wooden box-like compartment with a hinged door.

piano nobile the main floor of a house in which the reception rooms are situated. There is usually a ground floor or basement below and one or more upper floors, of lesser height, containing bedrooms.

piazza a square or rectangular open space surrounded on all sides by buildings. In England during the 17th and 18th centuries, the term was used inaccurately to describe a covered walkway, or ARCADE.

picturesque architecture the *picturesque* was a somewhat romantic idea of the late 1700s which, when applied to landscape, was associated with wild and dramatic features such as crags, waterfalls, rushing streams, gorges and natural woodland. Picturesque architecture was associated with small rustic cottages, castellated country houses and asymmetrical buildings or unusual combinations of forms set in the kind of landscape described above. The picturesque was popular with a number of architects during the early 1800s, notably John Nash.

pier or **pillar** a solid block of masonry or brick used to support an overlying structure, which is different from a COLUMN as it lacks the CAPITAL and BASE and other characteristics of the CLASSICAL ORDER. Often, a pier is square in section and it supports various overlying structures, e.g. an arch or lintel. The solid wall between such openings as doors and windows is called a *pier wall* or sometimes just a *pier*. A mirror hung on a pier wall is known as a *pier glass* and a table stood at the bottom is called a *pier table*. A *compound* or *clustered pier* is one with a core which is square in section ringed by several attached or detached shafts. (*See also* PILASTER).

various compound piers

pilaster a rectangular-shaped column which projects out slightly from a wall and conforms with an ORDER in CLASSICAL ARCHITECTURE.

portion of a decorated pilaster.

pillar *see* **pier**

pinnacle a small and narrow SPIRE on top of a PARAPET or BUTTRESS which is an ornamental feature. It is often

ornamented with *crockets* which are carved projections
of stone in a foliage design. These are a common feature
of GOTHIC architecture.

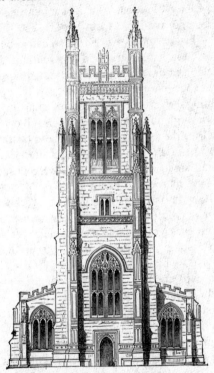

pinnacle ornamentation on St Neots Church

plaster used for lining both interior and exterior walls, has
been in use for many centuries and was much used by
Roman builders. In Britain in the Middle Ages, a combi-

nation of sand, lime and water was used as plaster, a variety of other ingredients being added for strength and to prevent cracking. These included feathers and animal hair, straw, hay, blood and dung. A much finer, tougher plaster became available from about 1260 onwards in England. This was *plaster of Paris,* so called because the gypsum used in its construction was found in the Montmartre region of the city. Since it was an imported item it was very expensive and was used in only the most important buildings. Eventually, sources of gypsum were discovered in England in the valleys of the rivers Nidd and Trent and on the Isle of Purbeck. The gypsum was extracted to make a type of ALABASTER called *English alabaster,* and smaller portions which were unsuitable for this were burnt for the manufacture of plaster. In 15th century Italy, Italian craftsmen began to work with a type of plaster or STUCCO which had been in use in Roman times. This was very fine and remained soft and easily worked for some time, drying slowly to produce a hard, strong plaster which was called *stucco duro.* As well as lime and gypsum, it additionally contained marble and was used for elaborate and fine decorative work. Various types of stucco for interior decoration were patented during the 1700s.

Also, experiments and improvements were made to stucco used on the external walls of buildings, particularly by John Nash (1752–1835). Cement began to be added to plaster for exterior work in the 1800s and different types were patented and in use by the 1840s. *Plasterboard*, consisting of a central layer of gypsum plaster sandwiched between external sheets of strong paper, began to be used after the First World War. This was due to the lack of skilled plasterers and this was even more apparent at the end of the Second World War. Plasterboard, which had been greatly improved during the intervening years, was widely adopted in post-war buildings and has remained in use ever since.

plinth the base of a PEDESTAL which is usually slightly larger or more projecting than the DADO and is moulded around the top.

ploughshare vault a type of vault in which the diagonal ribs arise at a lower level than the wall ribs, producing a pattern reminiscent of a ploughshare. It is also known as a *stilted* vault.

podium a continuous base or PLINTH which supports a series of columns or COLONNADE.

pointing mortar applied between the joints of bricks, masonry or stone which is normally flush with the surface of a wall (*flush pointing*). If slightly recessed, it is called *recessed pointing* and if deeply recessed, *hungry joint pointing*. If flush but grooved in the middle, it is known as *bag-rubbed pointing*.

poppy head a type of FINIAL or carved ornament at the top of the bench end of a PEW, usually in the form of an animal or human figure, foliage or *fleur de lis*.

porch a usually small, covered entrance to a building which is a feature in various guises of many different types of buildings and architectural styles. A grander and more ostentatious type of porch is known as a *portal*. One built wide enough to allow a wheeled vehicle to pass through is called a *porte cochère*. A *portico* is a roofed entrance supported by a classical COLONNADE. It may be

based on the style of a classical temple with a PEDIMENT or
have a different form such as a semi-circular plan.

a Romanesque porch

portcullis a defensive structure built into and guarding an
entrance to a CASTLE or other fortified building. It consists
of a grille of iron bars, or wood reinforced with iron, usually finishing in spikes at the base, which fit into vertical
slots on either side of the entrance. A portcullis could be
raised up and lowered quickly at times of danger or attack.

portico *see* **porch**.

Post-Modernism an architectural revolt against the ideas
of MODERNISM which first became current in the 1940s
and later in the 1960s and 70s. It has not resulted in any

particular architectural style but is rather a loose term which is applied to a variety of ideas.

postern, postern gate a small, unobtrusive gateway, often at the side or rear gate of a monastery, castle, palace, mansion or town. It may lead to a secret or concealed passageway.

prefabrication *see* **industrialized building**.

presbytery the part of a church containing the high altar situated at the east side of the choir and reserved for members of the clergy.

profile the outline of a moulding or, more universally, any part or the whole of a building.

pronaos an area behind the PORTICO and in front of the NAOS, with side walls which form a kind of ANTEROOM in a Greek TEMPLE. It is open to the PORTICO at the front.

propylaeum an entrance which may be a PORCH, gateway or VESTIBULE leading to a (usually sacred) enclosure such as the confines of a temple. The best known example is that of the Acropolis in Athens.

prostyle describing a Greek TEMPLE in which the COLUMNS of the PORTICO are in front of the PRONAOS.

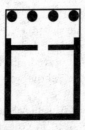

typical prostyle plan

pseudo-dipteral a type of Greek TEMPLE in which the PERISTYLE is formed from a double COLONNADE except around the walls of the NAOS where there is only a single row of COLUMNS.

pseudo-peripteral typically referring to a Roman TEMPLE, in which half columns are attached all round the external wall of the CELLA, in line with those of the PORTICO at the front. (*Compare* PERIPTERAL).

pteroma a passageway or AMBULATORY around a Greek TEMPLE sited between the PERISTYLE and the walls of the NAOS.

pulpit an elevated stand from which a minister or priest speaks to the congregation and preaches a sermon. He was known as an *ambo* in the early Medieval period, and the world pulpit came into use in the later part of the Middle Ages. The pulpit is made of wood or stone, often highly ornamented, decorated and carved and sometimes surmounted by an acoustic *sounding board*. Alternatively, there may be a decorative CANOPY or TESTER above a pulpit and it may be a free-standing structure or attached to a PIER or the wall of the NAVE. Sometimes a pulpit is attached to the external wall of a church for preaching to a larger congregation outside.

pulpitum a screen made of stone in a large church or cathedral, which divides the chancel from the nave. It is usually carved and decorated and may contain statues, supporting a GALLERY above or a CANOPY may be present.

Purbeck marble a type of limestone named after the Isle of Purbeck which is dark in colour and was used as a marble from the 12th and 13th centuries onwards. It was used especially for the construction of compound PIERS in churches, creating an effect of light and shade particularly in conjunction with other types of stone. It can be very highly polished and its other main use was in the sculpture of effigies.

pulvin a feature of Byzantine architecture which is a DOSSERET with a convex, rounded, pillow-like shape. It is an extra block of stone on top of the ABACUS of the CAPITAL.

purlin a horizontal timber which runs lengthways along a roof. There are a number of different kinds of purlin depending upon their position in the roof.

pylon a feature of the architecture of ancient Egypt being one of a pair of short towers with a rectangular base and pyramidal shape, set on either side of a temple gateway.

pylon at the Palace at Luxor

pyramid an enormous and massive structure with a square base and sloping sides which meet at a point at the top. Pyramids were a feature of ancient Egyptian building, constructed as tombs and monuments for important officials or members of the Royal family.

the pyramid of Ghizeh

Q

quadrangle a large oblong or square courtyard surrounded by buildings on all four sides and a feature of schools and universities.

quadrifrons a Roman structure with four arches and normally square in plan, placed at a crossroads.

quadriga a large sculpture of a chariot drawn by a row of four horses, placed on top of a building FAÇADE or monument.

quadripartite vault a type of VAULT in which the bay is divided into four compartments, due to the crossing over of two diagonal ribs.

quarrel a pane of glass in a medieval leaded window which was often painted. Also known as a *quarry*, it was usually diamond-shaped or as a square set on its point. The lead dividing the rods are called *canes*.

quoin one of a number of shaped or dressed stones at the corner of a building forming the external angle. The word is derived from the French *coin* meaning *angle* or *corner* and quoins are normally laid so that alternate ones show a large and then small face in the surface of each wall.

R

rabbet (or rebate) a rectangular step-like recess in a piece of wood or stone into which another piece closes or fits.

rafter a sloping beam of a roof which runs from the EAVE to the apex (ridge) to support the roof covering.

raggle a horizontal groove in a wall which accepts the edge of a roof, or more commonly the edge of a flashing which is then fixed with mortar.

ragstone a hard coarse stone used in masonry and the opposite to freestone which is fine grained and worked easily. Ragstone splits naturally along bedding or foliation planes into thin blocks that can easily be broken into the required size.

ragwork the use of RAGSTONE for building purposes. The stones are often laid flat with a thick layer of mortar in between and it may then be plastered and ROUGHCAST or pointed. The ragstone may also be laid in a herring-bone design.

rainwater head a metal box-like structure which is fixed to the upper end of a rainwater down-pipe and into which water is discharged from the gutter. It may be decorated and is usually made of iron or lead.

rampart a defensive wall around a castle, fortified city or similar construction built of earth, stone or brick.

random rubble *see* **rubble walling**.

rear arch the arch which spans a window or doorway on the inside of a wall.

rear vault the small vault situated between the inner face of a wall and the glass or tracery of a window created by the thickness of the wall itself. The glass is on the outer face, and on the inner is often a rib.

reeding a form of decoration comprising touching parallel convex mouldings.

Regency architecture specifically architecture during the years 1811–20 when George IV was Prince Regent, although in broader use it covers the period from the close of the 18th century until about 1830. It was a time in which past styles were again brought to the fore, but with modification. Changes occurred at a rapid pace and many new ideas were developed. In general, it was well-designed with modest decoration and examples include Lansdown Crescent in Bath (along classical lines) and All Saints' Church, London (Greek revival).

regular coarsed rubble *see* **rubble walling**.

reinforced concrete concrete that contains steel reinforcement to accommodate the tensile stresses created upon loading. The steel may be in the form of rods or mesh.

Renaissance architecture the Renaissance began in Italy (as *rinascimento*) during the 14th century and signified a return to the culture and motifs of ancient Rome. The term eventually came to be applied to architecture and covers the period from the early 1400s to the mid-1500s. The peak of Renaissance architecture in Italy was during the 16th century during which time numerous villas and palaces were built.

As the Renaissance spread westward through Europe, it lost much of its original quality and each country stamped upon the Italian renaissance its own style.

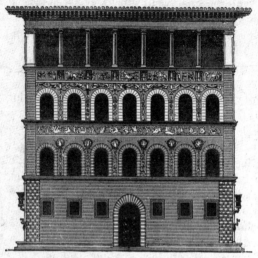

a Renaissance palace

In England the Renaissance manifested itself more as a form of decoration although tombs for Henry VII and Lady Margaret in Westminster Abbey exhibited Renaissance form. The purer Renaissance style in England was initiated by Inigo Jones at the start of the 17th century. He visited Italy and returned with much knowledge of Roman monuments and an appreciation of PALLADIAN architecture which is reflected in his later designs.

rendering plastering with render, a mortar or similar mix. Cement-based mortar is used for external walls as it is generally unaffected by dampness.

respond a half-PIER, often at the end of an ARCADE, bonded into a wall and which carries one end of an ARCH.

retaining wall a wall that is constructed to hold back a solid material, usually earth. Depending upon the design and way in which the wall works, it may be a *fixed* or *free* retaining wall. They are usually constructed of concrete, steel or timber. Also known as REVETEMENT.

reticulated the term applied to a net-like feature in a decoration or element of a building (*see* TRACERY).

return the point at which a feature such as a wall, moulding or dripstone continues at an angle to the original orientation. The same applies to a down-pipe which changes orientation on the face of a wall. It also describes the choir stalls that are positioned against the screen at the west end of the choir.

reveal the part of the JAMB, in a door or window opening, that can be seen and which is not covered by the frame.

revetement another term for a retaining wall, but also the cladding (e.g. marble) fixed to a wall constructed of a different material.

rib a band, on a ceiling or vault, which is raised and may be structural and/or decorative. Ribs are often used to ornament ceilings especially when vaulted and groined. Throughout the various styles groins are usually covered by ribs and the rib intersections are decorated, for example with bosses. In the more decorative architectural styles there are often additional ribs, other than those that follow the groins (diagonals) and those that cross the vault at right angles (cross-springers). Such complex arrangements may lead to a tracery effect, often further decorated.

ribbon development the building of houses in a narrow strip along both sides of a main road, the latter often being new. This was very common in Britain during the inter-war years but such development was heavily restricted by an Act of Parliament in 1935.

ridge rib the main rib along the ridge of a VAULT which may run either along the length or the width.

rise the vertical distance between the level of the springing line and the SOFFIT of the crown of an arch or vault.

rococo the rococo is a decorative style which formed the last phase of the Baroque. It originated in France and created a contrast to the heavy, imposing style of the Baroque. Rococo is typified by lightness and interiors exhibit an asymmetrical and often abstract form utilizing ribbons, scrolls, shells, flowers and trees, country scenes and possibly Chinese motifs. Colours were generally pastel shades. Rococo exteriors were plain and simple with basic ornaments. The style is essentially absent in England save for some interior designs.

decorative detail from the time of Louis XIV

decorative details from the time of Louis XV

Roman architecture the use of rounded elements such as domes, vaults and arches is prevalent in Roman architecture and the use of bricks with concrete enabled all these elements and walls to be built to significant proportions. A stunning example was the Pantheon which featured a

dome 140 feet in diameter. The BASILICA is a typical example of Roman building as are the AMPHITHEATRE and the
TRIUMPHAL ARCH. Most great Roman buildings were concrete faced with brick or reticulated masonry which consisted of small, diamond-shaped tiles or stones.

Roman domestic architecture fell broadly into three
types—the country house or VILLA, TOWNHOUSES or *domus*
and the apartment or *insula*. Villas were built for wealthy
men and were extensive, covering a large site. Town
houses were for the middle classes and presented only a narrow, street frontage, but extended some distance back on a
rectangular ground plan. The apartment or insula was a
multi-storey construction containing numerous flats and
which could be built with four or more storeys, although
two was more common. These were basic living units often with shops on the ground floor and the blocks were constructed around squares or symmetrically along streets.

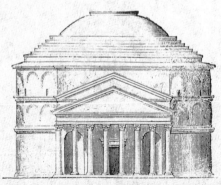

the Pantheon at Rome

Roman baths formed an essential part of Roman life providing a social, leisure and bathing facility. In addition
citizens could obtain food and drink, medical treatment,
undertake business or participate in sporting events.
Baths built for emperors were very impressive and extensive, incorporating several large halls and rooms, many
of which had barrel-vaulted ceilings, which with the
walls were highly decorated.

ornamented vaulted roof with panels

Romanesque architecture preceded the Gothic style and
consisted of attempts to imitate the features of Roman architecture. As such arches are round, supporting pillars
retain a classical proportion, walls are thick and windows
are small.

The onset of the Romanesque style varies within Europe and two types evolved, one in the north and west, and another in central Europe. The latter followed more closely the Roman style with round arches, tunnel vaults, etc. and churches showed the basilican plan. Romanesque architecture of north and west Europe showed less influence from the Roman style and in England during the 11th century, the Normans built massive walls in castles and churches to allow for poor mortar, wide joints and generally inferior construction methods. In time, the constructions became finer and ornamentation increased and some excellent examples were built, such as most of Durham Cathedral, and the naves of certain cathedrals, e.g. Ely.

Romanesque ornamentation began in simple fashion with mouldings sparsely decorated but this became more decorative in the later stages. In Britain the later form was commonly geometric with chevrons or herring-bone patterns. Towards the end of the 12th century, prominent sculptured decoration adorned doorways and capitals and consisted of flowers, animals, human and mythical forms.

rood a cross, usually wooden, and comes from the Saxon word for a crucifix or cross. In churches it was placed on a beam stretching from one RESPOND to another of the chancel arch at the east end of the nave with figures of the Virgin and St. John on either side. Occasionally it was painted on the wall over the chancel arch.

rood loft a gallery, approached by either wooden stairs or stairs built into the wall, above the ROOD SCREEN for the purpose of carrying the ROOD, candles or other images.

They were introduced in the 15th century but many of them were destroyed during the Reformation.

rood screen a screen which shut off the chancel as it was placed across the east end of the nave below the ROOD.

roof the outer upper covering of any building which can be made of many different materials and designed to one of numerous configurations. A fundamental property of a roof is the *pitch* which is the angle between the horizontal and the line of the roof. A roof's highest point is the ridge and the lowest is the EAVES. Roofs are usually symmetric with a central ridge, but can be asymmetric with an offset ridge or have one pitching plane (monopitch). A *North light* roof is asymmetric and the steep part of the roof is glazed and faces north to give uniform lighting. The *mansard* is a symmetric roof with two distinct slopes on either side of the ridge, the part at the eaves having a much greater pitch. Mansard roofs are useful in that they increase the usable roof space and glazing can be fixed in the lower part. Barrel vaults and domes are both forms of curved roofs. The *hip* of a roof is the sloping corner where the sloping end of a roof meets the sloping sides and this can be used to reduce the height of a gable wall. A *helm roof* has four faces meeting at a point, each face also possessing a gable (as in a spire shape).

A roof may also be defined by the main structural element. A single framed roof has no main trusses while a *double-framed roof* has longitudinal members supported by principal rafters. *Hammerbeam roof*, e.g. Westminster House, uses hammerbeams (horizontal supports at the wall) to support the timbers and a central vertical timber between ridge and a supporting beam produce a *king-*

post roof. All the components and elements of a roof structure have this individual terminology, such as braces (subsidiary timbers to strengthen the frame), collar beam (horizontal timbers connecting rafters) and purlins (horizontal timbers running along the length of the roof, carrying rafters and providing support).

rose window a round window ornamented with foils of patterned tracery giving the effect of spokes of a wheel.

rose window in the Church of St Croix at Orleans

rotunda a circular building or room, often domed and surrounded by a colonnade. A Roman example of this is the Pantheon.

roughcast an external rendering applied as two coats of a mixture of cement and sand. Before the second coat is dry, crushed stone, gravel or pebbles are thrown on to it. Also known as *pebbledash*.

rubble walling a style of coarse walling generally consisting of rough stones of irregular size and not necessarily flat bedded. In many cases, rubble walling was faced with better material or bonded with thick mortar and pointed. There are several types of rubble walling depending upon the stones used and the method of laying.

Stones of varying sizes laid without any obvious pattern create *random rubble* while *coursed random rubble* has irregular shaped stones laid in horizontal layers. Square stones laid in courses form *regular coursed rubble* while *square-snecked rubble* is the use of generally rectangular faced blocks with small stone blocks (snecks) to break long vertical joints.

rustication massive blocks of masonry used to give a striking effect to exterior walls, usually the power part. The blocks (sometimes in a basic quarry-dressed state) are divided by deep joints and different effects are used: *banded*, only the horizontal joints are emphasized; *chamfered*, smooth stones divided by V joints (as in *smooth*); *cyclopean* (or *rock-faced*) very large blocks directly from the quarry (or carved to give the same effect); *diamond-pointed,* each stone cut as a low pyramid; *frosted*, the surface is carved to give the effect of icicles; *smooth,* blocks are finished with a level surface and chamfered edges

emphasizing the joints; *vermiculated,* a worm track effect
is given by the blocks being carved with wavy channels. It is
occasionally copied in stucco or other compositions.

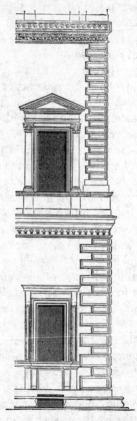

an example of rustication on a Renaissance palace

S

sacristy a church room in which the sacred items (vessels, vestments and any valuable items) were stored. Also the room in which the priest robed (otherwise known as the vestry).

saddleback roof a pitched roof over a tower.

sala terrena a feature of palaces in the 17th and 18th centuries in which a room on the ground floor opened onto a garden.

sally-port a POSTERN gate or passage which owes its origin to the passageway used by troops when going out to make a sally from a fortified building. In general architectural usage it is the entrance of a subterranean passage which joins parts of a castle or palace.

sanctuary the eastern part of the choir of a church and the area around the main altar, also known as the presbytery.

sash window a window consisting of two sashes, i.e. glazed frames of wood, metal or plastic, fixed into frames which permit the sashes to slide vertically. The two sashes remain in place when opened due to weights (of iron or lead) that are concealed in the frame of the window. Alternatively, there are sash balances which comprise a spring-loaded device.

satellite town a town that relies upon a larger nearby centre for certain facilities such as hospitals. This enables a population to be established at a new site and it was developed quite extensively in Scandinavia, beginning in the late 1940s.

Saxon architecture this is the architecture prior to the Norman Conquest but is found to belong to two distinct periods, from the 7th and early 8th centuries and then the 10th and early 11th. A great deal of the earlier construction and culture was destroyed during the raids of the Vikings in the intervening periods.

The buildings initially were usually constructed in wood and wattle and daub but there is evidence to show that ecclesiastical buildings were made of stone, most likely irregular rubble work with ashlar stones at the corners. The earlier Saxon architecture centres on two areas, one in the south and one in the north, in Kent and Northumbria respectively. Churches built in the south during this period took certain features from Rome although, in general, they were of a simpler design. Northumbrian churches showed Celtic features although late in the 7th century a number of Roman features could be found, e.g. barrel-vaulted crypts.

The second phase of Saxon architecture features both new building and some rebuilding and most Saxon (or Anglo-Saxon) architecture seen today is from this period. A typical decorative architectural feature is PILASTER strips which are seen particularly on towers as *lesene* (pilaster without capital or base). Other typical features include walls of rag or rubble, without buttresses, with QUOINS placed flat and then on end to produce an effect called *long and short*. The towers also show a characteristic style with vertical stone strips projecting from the face of the wall slightly, and often these are in tiers joined by bands or crude arches.

Doorways and other openings also display long and short work with projecting stonework over the opening. Windows tend to be small, with round or pointed heads and double lights are divided by a BALUSTER shaft. There are a number of churches from this period exhibiting such features, e.g. the church of St. Lawrence at Bradford-on-Avon, and remains of the earlier style are seen in the crypt at Hexham Abbey Church.

scaffold a temporary framework that provides a platform and access for exterior work on buildings, e.g. bricklaying, pointing, cleaning, painting. The tubular versions are made of steel or aluminium and clip together and anchor to the building. The vertical poles are called standards, horizontal poles, ledgers.

scagliola a material used to imitate marble which was used by the Romans and later in England, Italy and elsewhere. It consists of gypsum, isinglass, glue and sometimes fragments of marble. The resulting compound was hard and could be polished. In 16th century Italy it was used for table tops among other things, and in England during the 17th and 18th centuries it was popular for floors, table tops, decorative inlay and other purposes.

scallop the shell-like shape of an ornament, carving or moulding.

sconce a small earthwork or fort built for military purposes to defend a castle gate, pass or similar structure or feature.

scotia a hollow moulding used frequently in the bases of columns in classical architecture and which, due to its curvature, casts a strong shadow.

Scottish architecture the effect of the Roman occupation on Scotland was quite superficial leaving its mark through a number of forts and monuments such as the Antonine Wall. Prior to this construction encompassed stone circles, chambered tombs, round houses and BROCHS. BEEHIVE construction then featured after the Romans and then from the 10th century Scotland was touched by the various styles and impressive buildings were constructed during the Romanesque (11th century) and Norman (12th century) influences. The Gothic is well represented in certain cathedrals and abbeys but in the 15th and 16th centuries, secular architecture developed more. The Renaissance affected the style of decoration applied to many elements or rooms of major castles built in the 16th century; however Scotland comes to the fore with its Elizabethan and Jacobean tower houses.

London style filtered through to Scotland in the late 17th century and Georgian styles are very similar and Adam designed many Scottish castles in the 18th century. In the 1830s, William Burn began the style known as Scottish Baronial, for country houses and his pupil Bryce became well known for this design. By the 1890s, Scotland had an architect who would be known throughout Europe and whose influence would be felt many years later—Charles Rennie Mackintosh. He merged art nouveau with an angular design to create a movement still reflected today.

screen a wooden or stone partition, which may have doors, that separated a part of a room or church from the rest. In halls of the Middle Ages the screen was often at the entrance and enclosed a small entrance lobby, with gallery above and entrance to the hall itself was thus through a door in the screen.

In churches, screens fulfilled various functions: enclosing the choir, separating smaller chapels and so on (*see also* ROOD SCREEN). Early English screens are usually stone and ornamented with panels and possibly open arches above the mid-point. Many perpendicular screens in churches display ornamentation including statues, panelling, pinnacles, carvings and tracery.

screens passage a corridor-like space in a medieval hall which was separated from the hall by a decorated screen. It was often at the same end of the hall as the services, the kitchen, pantry and buttery, and it prevented draughts entering the hall and gave a route by which food could be taken from the kitchen to the hall. Often a gallery would be constructed above and the main entrance of the hall could open into the screens passage.

scroll a type of ornamentation consisting of convoluted shapes, similar to a partly rolled scroll of paper. It also refers to the moulding of this shape found in Early English or Decorated architecture.

sedile a seat, found particularly in churches, and usually made of stone and set into the wall. There are many of the Perpendicular period and they usually consist of three seats. Around the recess is often found pinnacles and other decoration. The seats are usually set in the south side of the chancel, near the altar, and were used by the priest and attendants during the services.

set-off a feature, seen particularly with buttresses, whereby a wall or element is reduced in thickness creating a planar ledge, often sloping, between the two thicknesses. Set-offs are often covered (*see* SKEW) or obscured by mouldings. Sloping set-offs have a DRIP to throw off water.

severy a bay of a VAULT.

sexpartite vault a type of VAULT in which a bay of a QUADRIPARTITE VAULT is further divided into two by a transverse division.

shaft the part of a column or pillar between the CAPITAL and the base. It is used especially to describe small columns around a pillar or columns in door jambs or window surrounds. They may be part of the same stone as the pillar to which they are attached or they can be separated pieces. Sections vary in shape and are often ornamented.

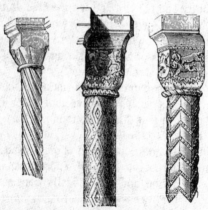

ornamented shafts

shingle a tile made of wood, usually oak, and cut to a specific size for covering roofs, spires and walls. Shingles were used from Roman times to the Middle Ages whereupon they were replaced by clay tiles.

sill the timber or stone which is set horizontally at the foot of a window or doorway or similar opening. Into it are set the vertical members of the opening, and the sill projects beyond the face of the wall to throw off water.

skew in general terms and usage, oblique or slanting. Referring specifically to a building element it is the part which is at an angle to the rest of the structure, for example, the coping of a gable or the stones forming the slopes of the SET-OFFS of buttresses. It may also refer precisely to the stone at the bottom of a gable that supports coping stones above.

skirting a board, usually wooden, set at the base of a wall (fixed vertically to the wall) to protect the wall surface.

skylight a window set into a roof (and also called a rooflight) to provide top-lighting. It may open, be fixed or be simply a rooflight sheet. Variations on the basic window include the barrel vault ridge light which is a curved, translucent assembly fixed at the ridge; domed rooflights which may be square, or circular lights raised above roof level on a narrow kerb.

skyscraper a very tall, multi-storey building constructed upon a steel framework, *see* HIGH-RISE BUILDING.

slate a fine-grained metamorphic rock (formed by the effect of heat and pressure upon sediments such as clay, shale etc.) with a pronounced fissility enabling it to be cleaved into thin sheets for use in building and mainly for roofing. It can also be used, in greater thicknesses, for stairs, paving, shelves or more ornamental elements.

Due, however, to its durability and non-porous nature, it has been used extensively for roofing since Roman times. Its popularity has fallen and risen again and it came back into use during the Middle Ages. Welsh slate is particularly renowned and this originates from the late 18th century when the smooth slate was in great demand to satisfy the increased rate of building as towns developed.

Slate-hanging is an alternative use for this material in which a wall is covered with overlapping slates fastened onto wooden supports. In the 1600s and throughout the 1700s, this was a popular means of cladding walls and ultimately became decorative as well as functional as shaped slates were used.

sleeper wall a wall that carries the joists of a timber ground floor. Also a wall that supports SLEEPERS or is built between two structural elements such as walls or piers, to prevent movement.

sleeper (or beam) a horizontal timber that supports floor or ceiling joists.

slype a covered passage in a cathedral from the cloisters and between the transept and chapterhouse.

soffit the underside of any element within a building, be it a floor, arch, balcony, vault, staircase.

solar a private room on the first or second floor of a house, particularly in the 14th to 16th centuries, to which the family could retire. It was usually at the same end of the hall as the daïs and reached by a staircase from it. There could be a cellar beneath the solar and these together often did not occupy the full height of the great hall. The solar also frequently had a small window through which the lord or other occupants could view the proceedings in the great hall below.

solomonic column a column, believed to have originated from Solomon's temple, which is fluted or shaped in a spiral fashion.

space frame a three-dimensional structure that can be designed to span large spaces with few or no supporting columns that intervene. The component elements of the structure are interconnected and act as one structure, resisting loads from all directions. Space frames, or space structures, include domes, tent structures and others and some have an external appearance resembling an egg box.

span the distance between the supports of a roof, arch, bridge etc.

spandrel the near triangular space between the arch of a doorway and the rectangle around it which may be formed by a moulding. It is also applied to other similar spaces such as between arches, or the surface of a vault between RIBS. The spandrels are then often ornamented with tracery, foliage and similar features.

a decorated spandrel in a Church porch

spire the pointed top of a tower, roof or turret which usually reaches a considerable height. Early spires of the
12th century were of limited height and corresponded in
their base plan with the plan of the tower upon which
they were built, thus a circular tower had a circular
(conic) spire.

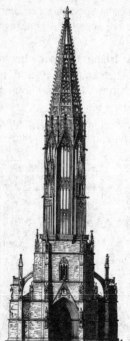

a church with an octagonal spire

In the Early English period spires acquired greater eleva-
tion and most were octagonal in section, with pinnacles

or masonry covering the corners of the tower not occupied by the spire base. This is a *broach* spire where there is no intermediate parapet and which employed SQUINCHES across the corners to support the other sides. Spires of the Decorated style were *needle* spires, and in addition to their slenderness they possessed a greater degree of enrichment and often decorated flying buttresses. As in the Perpendicular style, such towers had a parapet allowing room at the base of the spire to walk and erect a scaffold for repair work.

Spires were made of stones or wood covered with lead or SHINGLES.

splay the sloping edge around a doorway or window which expands the opening along the depth of the wall. It is typical of Gothic architecture.

spur has numerous uses in architectural terminology: a supporting strut; a sloping buttress; an ornamental carved feature, often foliage, that is found between the plinth and the circular base moulding above; and a projection from a wall that has some protective purpose.

spur stone a stone that projects from or is erected at the corner of a building or arch to prevent passing traffic creating damage to the element.

square-snecked rubble *see* **rubble walling**

squinch *see* **dome**

squint an opening cut at an angle through the wall of a church or through a pier to enable a view of the altar to be gained when it would not otherwise be possible. This was applicable to views from the aisle or the transepts. Squints are usually plain but can be ornamented. Another term for them is hagioscope.

staddle stones stones shaped like mushrooms upon which are supported wooden structures such as hay barns or granaries. Raising the structure on the stones helps minimise damp and prevent damage by rodents.

stadium in the time of the ancient Greeks this was a running track, the name being derived from the unit of measure, stade (about 600 ft). In time, the stadium was used for wider athletics events and also for drama and music. Most stadia were unroofed and constructed set into a hillside. In modern usage a stadium is used for sporting and non-sporting events of all kinds that require a large audience capacity. Modern designs are usually constructed from steel, reinforced concrete with plastics for certain elements.

stained glass *see* **glass**

staircase staircases appear to have existed as long as architecture and over the ages there has been an infinite variety of style. An extensive terminology is attached to staircases, with names for the various parts. The horizontal part of the step is the *tread*, and the vertical part is the *riser*. If the tread overhangs the riser, the overhang is called the *nosing*, and if a tread is wider at one end, it is called a *winder*. The *newel* is the main post at the end of a staircase and attached to it is the *handrail* and to the latter are connected the *balusters*, vertical rails attached at their base to the tread or the *string* (a vertical board attached to the edge of the stairs).

There are several configurations of staircase. A spiral (winding, turnpike or newel) staircase has a central post to which the stairs are attached and around which they wind upwards. A single flight of stairs with no turns is a straight stair. One turn through ninety degrees with a landing in between the two flights of stair is a quarter turn with landing, and a dog-leg stair is two flights parallel to each other and offset by a landing. There are other variations combining these features, or utilising winders to negotiate corners.

From simple beginnings thousands of years ago, the importance of staircases in the overall design of a building has changed appreciably. In the Middle Ages, the spiral staircase was the most common. Made of wood or stone, it was often built into the thickness of stone walls or in a tower or turret. Another method was to have an external flight of stone stairs, or an internal wooden flight, commonly with no risers. Single flight staircases became common as internal features during the 15th century and in the late 1500s the dog-leg stair was introduced and this was used in the great houses of the Elizabethan period. In due course, the dog-leg design was developed further to form the open-well staircase in which the stairs were adjacent to the walls of a well, leaving a hole from top to bottom of the well. Many such staircases were constructed in the 17th century, often of wood and ornamented with carved balusters and other decorations. During the 1700s and 1800s there was a tremendous variety of design and use of materials and often a very high degree of craftsmanship. Modern staircases, by comparison, have tended to revert to simpler styles reflecting the mass production of recent times.

stall the division of a stable into compartments for animals. Also, and more relevant architecturally, a fixed seat in a church or cathedral, usually covered partially at the back and/or sides. The seat would be one of several in a row and be made of stone or more commonly wood, and used by the clergy or choir in the church. Often the stalls feature panelling to the rear, carved ends to the rows and short desks or shelves to the front. Additional embellishments were common in the larger churches and cathedrals with tracery, pinnacles and similar elements.

On the underneath of the seats in stalls are often found projecting brackets. The seats are hinged and when turned up the brackets provide a little support when standing for a long time. The brackets are called *misericords* (originally miserere) and were usually carved with foliage, animals and so on.

stanchion a vertical supporting element or strut, usually made of steel and previously of cast iron. Previously the term applied to bars around a tomb or the iron bar between the mullions of a window.

stay a structural diagonal bars, trace or strut used to prevent movement in a structure.

steel frame construction the principle of design and construction whereby a building framework of interconnected steel sections provides a load carrying frame upon which the remainder can be built in brick and other materials. The rolled steel sections are welded or bolted together.

The use of steel in building became possible when Bessemer and Siemens both developed techniques for the production of cheaper, purer steel during the first half of the 19th century. Bessemer's process involved blowing a stream of air through the furnace, and Siemens used the heat from waste gases to preheat the components entering the furnace. The Bessemer process was developed further into the open-hearth method and by the turn of the 20th century, this was the primary method of steel making.

More recent methods are now used, and a tremendous range of alloy steels is available for particular uses. For construction purposes, the steels must have a high tensile strength for use in multi-storey buildings.

steeple the tower and SPIRE of a church.

stellar vault an ornate vault in which a star-shaped pattern is created by the intersecting RIBS, LIERNES and TIERCERONS.

stone the traditional material used in masonry consisting of cut rock such as limestone, sandstone or marble. Chosen for its durability and architectural qualities it can be carved, used as structural elements, decorative features or purely functional components such as paving.

When stone was first used, it could not be transported great distances hence the buildings which utilised it were in the vicinity of the source. Also the cost of quarrying and working the stone were such that only wealthy clients could afford stone buildings.

Now there is great variety in the stone used—stone being a general term to describe quarried building material whether it is a stone or not, geologically. Limestones and sandstones are commonest and both are sedimentary rocks, formed by deposition of calcareous and siliceous grains respectively. Marble is limestone that has been subjected to heat and has recrystallized into a hard stone. Granite is also used extensively and this is a coarse, crystalline igneous rock formed by the slow cooling at depth of molten rock. Granite and marble are often finished with a high polish while limestone and sandstone can be carved.

Among the various 'stones' available for building are:

Bath stone: an oolitic limestone (composed of cemented ooids which are concentric rings of calcium carbonate on a nucleus formed from a grain) used widely for hundreds of years.

Carboniferous limestone: a fairly widespread limestone often highly fossiliferous found in the Pennines, Mendips and the Derbyshire Peak District.

Chalk: a form of limestone, very fine grained, composed of skeletal remains from micro-organisms. It is found particularly on the south coast of England.

Clipsham limestone: a hard, creamy coloured stone from Lincolnshire.

Connemara marble: a dolomitic limestone (containing magnesium as well as calcium carbonate) from Ireland, one of the few marbles in the UK and Eire.

Cotswold stone: a limestone used widely since the Middle Ages.

Granite: a crystalline igneous rock containing quartz (translucent), feldspar (pink or white) and mica (translucent, and black/brown) which on polishing gives a very attractive finish. Granite is often used to clad buildings because it is resistant to weathering and pollution and this is particularly apparent in the 'Granite City' of Aberdeen.

Marlstone: a ferruginous limestone from the Midlands and used a lot in the Middle Ages.

Millstone Grit: a coarse sandstone from the Pennines and other areas, which although durable can often be friable.

Old Red Sandstone: an attractive sandstone from Scotland, Wales and Devon and Cornwall which was deposited under terrestrial conditions. The rock may have a red, brown, purple or pink colour.

Portland stone: a very well-known building stone from the Isle of Portland in Dorset. It is the most widely used stone in Britain, some way ahead of Bath stone and others, principally because of its fine, even texture which, when suitable saws became available in the 17th century, allowed large blocks to be cut. Wren used Portland stone extensively in rebuilding the City of London.

Purbeck marble: this is actually a limestone from Dorset and was very popular in the Middle Ages, particularly for column shafts in churches.

There are other stones such as Ancaster, Weldon, Ham Hill which are good limestones; Craigleith, a sandstone used extensively in Edinburgh; Wealden, a sandstone from Sussex and many more, including the sandstones York, Darley Dale, Lazenby, Dumfries and Stoke Hall.

Another method of using stone for building is in natural stone-faced units in which cut pieces of a particular stone are bonded to a concrete carrier unit. This technique allows the production of precisely detailed units combined with the benefits of natural stone. Granite, limestone and sandstone are commonly used but marble and slate are also suitable.

stops the stones against which features such as hoodmoulds end. They are often carved and project from the wall.

storey a vertical division of a building and the space between two floors. In the UK, the storey below ground level is the basement, followed by the ground floor (first

floor in America). The first floor in the past was called
the principal floor and the second, third, etc floors followed. The rooms on the top floor might have sloping
ceilings with dormer windows in which case they would
be called attics.

Storeys that are intermediate, say at a level between
ground and first floors, are called mezzanines or entresols.

strapwork a surface ornamentation on ceilings, panelling
and friezes which became popular in the Netherlands in
the 16th century and spread to England. It consists of interlaced decorated bands with mouldings at the edges of
the bands.

street furniture a general term to encompass the items
seen on streets, such as railings, litter bins, lampposts,
telephone kiosks, park benches and so on.

stressed skin construction a method of construction in
which an outer skin is fastened to a framework to form an
integrated unit. The whole unit then acts as one in terms
of its flexural strength. Timber is generally used in this
way but plastics and metals may be suitable. The terminology derives from the aircraft industry.

strut a structural element, often timber and commonly
found in roofs, that prevents two other elements from
moving towards each other. The strut is therefore under
compression.

stucco a material of unknown origin which was developed
by the Romans for decorating ceilings. It is essentially a
slow-setting plaster composed of gypsum, sand and
slaked lime (calcium hydroxide) and additives to enhance durability and other properties. It was also used by
Islamic architects both internally and externally and dur-

ing the Renaissance it was used extensively for interior decoration, e.g. Fontainebleau. The use of stucco in Germany during the 17th and 18th centuries became very elegant and elaborate and was commonly combined with boiseries (wood panelling).

Stucco in England described a slightly different material which contained marble dust to bind and strengthen. It also encompassed fine plasters which were used for internal decoration but also for external rendering or architectural features.

Joseph Rose was well known in the late 18th century for his work with stucco and he made numerous ceilings designed by the Adam brothers.

studs secondary vertical timbers in the walls of timber-framed buildings.

stylobate the base structure upon which a colonnade stands, or the top step of the stepped base (or crepidoma) of a Greek temple.

summerhouse *see* **gazebo**.

T

tabernacle a decorative NICHE or RECESS with a CANOPY in which the Holy sacraments are placed. Also, an ornamental receptacle containing the Holy sacraments, which may be in the form of a miniature church. The recess is usually situated above or behind the altar.

temenos the sacred area around a TEMPLE.

template a block of stone set at the top of a rubble wall or brick PIER to support and spread the weight of overlying BEAMS or JOISTS. Also, a pattern for cutting out shapes, or a mould.

temple a sacred building constructed for the purpose of worship and containing a statue of a god. In contrast to a Christian church, which is designed for the accommodation of a congregation of worshippers, the purpose of a classical temple was to house the image of a deity. Worshippers remained outside. The earliest plan of a Greek temple, based on Mycenaean architecture, was in the form of a rectangle with a colonnaded frontal porch. This led to a later plan of a PORTICO at either end and a central room, called the NAOS, in which the statue of the god was placed, with columns all the way round. Later still, a second smaller room was added, the OPISTHODOMUS, which served as a treasury for gifts.

The number of columns in the portico varied according to the size of the temple. *Tetrastyle* had four, *hexastyle* had six, *octastyle* had eight, *decastyle* had ten and *dodecastyle* had twelve. The temple was supported on a raised platform called the STYLOBATE with a three-stepped base leading up to it called the *crepidoma*. There were no windows but light entered through doorways and skylights set into the roof. The roof itself was tiled and low pitched, with guttering and occasional waterspouts, called ANTEFIXAE. The roof ended in a PEDIMENT above the PORTICO at either end and this was enriched at the ends and apex by ornaments, figures or statues called ACROTERIA. The face of the pediment, or TYMPANUM and the FRIEZE were usually decorated with carving and sculpture or painted. The naos was left plain and sunlight shining through the doorway in the east wall illuminated the statue of the god. In the larger temples there were two tiers of columns running lengthways which divided the interior and supported the roof.

Roman temples were based on the Greek design but somewhat modified to accommodate the needs and customs of worship. The chamber where the figure of the deity was housed was called the CELLA and this was longer and wider than the Greek naos. Often it was enlarged to such an extent as to eliminate altogether the PERISTYLE on the long sides and rear of the temple. The columns or rather half-columns were attached to the external walls of the cella in line with those of the front portico. This arrangement is called *pseudo-peripteral* and *peripteral* describes a temple surrounded by free-standing columns. A larger central space was needed in Roman temples to house a greater quantity of treasure, much of it brought from Greece itself. Roman temples were normally supported on a PODIUM which was reached by a flight of steps at the front of the portico. In contrast, some Roman temples like the Temple of Vesta in Rome were circular in plan and encircled by a ring of free-standing columns.

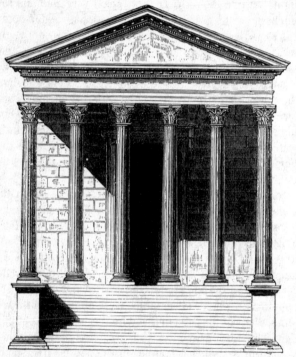

the temple at Nismes

tenia a type of small, thin fillet moulding separating the ARCHITRAVE from the FRIEZE in the Greek Doric order (*see* CLASSICAL ORDER).

term, termini, terminal figure a PEDESTAL which is wider
at the top than at the base and so tapering downwards. At
the top it is carved into a figure which may be animal,
mythical or human, or it may carry a sculptured bust (*see*
CARYATID).

terrace a row of houses attached to and adjoining one another and planned and built as one unit. In the 1700s terraces were usually constructed in the PALLADIAN or neo-
classical style. Later, in the Victorian period, some were
built in a plainer, more utilitarian manner to provide
housing in the cities for a rapidly expanding population.

  The city of Bath was the birthplace of terrace architecture in Britain, brought about by its popularity as a spa
resort from the 1720s onwards. The main architect involved in the replanning and expansion of Bath was John
Wood (1704–54). He was able to visualize the city as a
whole and was, perhaps appropriately, very much influenced by the city's Roman architectural heritage. He
built using Bath stone, thereby helping to re-establish its
popularity. His work was carried on and expanded by the
next generation of architects including his son, also
called John Wood. They built magnificent terraces and
curving crescents of houses up the hillsides surrounding
the city centre. The most notable of these, the Royal
Crescent, was constructed between 1767 and 1775 and
was the work of John Wood, the younger. The terrace architecture of Bath was tremendously influential on the
development of other cities and towns throughout Britain
during the late 1700s and 1800s. Some grand sea-front
terraces were built during the 19th century, most notably
those constructed between 1800 and 1850 at Brighton

and Hove, the towns which owed their popularity to the patronage of the Prince Regent. By the middle of the 19th century, terrace building was well established and popular as an efficient and economical means of providing housing for the expanding populations of towns and cities. The style and quality of the buildings varied greatly depending upon the class and level of affluence of those for whom the houses were intended. However, the terraced house has retained its popularity through to the present day.

terracotta fired, earthenware clay which was introduced into Britain during the 1500s from Italy and was used mainly for decorative purposes. It is hard, relatively nonporous and used without glaze.

terrazzo a type of hard finish for walls and floors consisting of chips of marble set into cement and laid in situ. When dry, the surface is ground and polished.

tesserae small cubes or blocks of glass, marble or stone used to make a mosaic covering for a wall or floor. A surface in which tesserae are embedded is described as *tessellated*.

tester a CANOPY which may be hung from the ceiling or carried by wall supports and is situated above a PULPIT, throne, tomb, bed or other structure.

thatch a roof of straw, heather, reeds etc. held in place by stones, poles or wires. It is a type of roof which has existed for hundreds of years but has become increasingly rare in recent times.

theatre a building constructed for the purpose of staging an entertainment, such as a play or other event. A theatre must have enough space to stage the event and provide seating for a large audience. Ancient theatres were usually open to the air but those built in Europe in later centuries were normally enclosed and roofed.

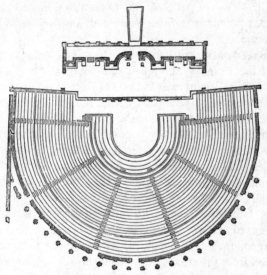

ground-plan of the theatre at Pompeii

tholos a circular building from ancient Greece which had a beehive-shaped central chamber and a conical or domed roof.

tierceron a secondary RIB in a VAULT which arises from the vault and springs to the RIDGE RIB.

tiles glazed tiles originating in the Near East were used for decorative purposes on floors and walls for many hundreds of years, and there are European examples dating from the 7th century AD. Later they were used very extensively for the decoration of both the inside and outside walls of mosques. More recently they were popular for the decoration of external walls by architects interested in the ideas of Art Nouveau. Ornamental glazed tiles remain popular for the decoration of internal walls in the present day.

Baked or fired tiles for roofs, floors and walls were used by the Romans throughout the Empire. Their use declined in Britain after the end of Roman occupation and began again at some point during the Middle Ages. They were often made with bricks in brick kilns and, along with stone tiles, became popular for roofing in towns during this period as they were less of a fire hazard. Floor tiles were also popular during the Middle Ages and these were sometimes decorated. Tile covering of external walls, known as *weather tiling* or *tile-hanging*, began in the late 1600s, especially in the south of England. Designs of tiles and patterns varied, so that these were partly ornamental, although the main purpose was to protect the wall from the effects of rain and snow. The tiles were attached to wooden battens fastened to the walls or nailed into the mortar. Slates were similarly used (*slate-hanging*) in the north of England.

Brick tiles, *weather tiles* or *mathematical tiles* were commonly used on exterior walls especially during the years 1760 to 1830. These were about the same size as bricks and were attached to a wall as in tile hanging. They were useful for weather protection but their main purpose was to disguise the wall and give it a more up-to-date appearance according to the fashion of the time. A *plain* or *plane* tile is an ordinary flat tile whereas a *pan-*

tile is a large one with an s-shaped curved profile. These were introduced into Britain in the 1630s from Flanders and used for roofing, but were made in England from the 1700s onwards. *Encaustic tiles* are a glazed, ornamental type used on walls and floors in the Middle Ages, and were also popular during the 1800s. A *harmus tile* is one which lies over and conceals a joint between other tiles. A Roman roof was sometimes covered by flat tiles called *tegulae* (singular *tegula*) which alternated with rounded ones called *imbrices* (singular *imbrex*) that concealed the joints.

timber framing a timber-framed building is one which has a framework of vertical and horizontal timbers, the intervening spaces being infilled with other materials. This might be BRICKWORK (*see* NOGGING), PLASTER (*see* PARGETING), wattle and daub or wooden boarding (*see* CLAPBOARD and WEATHERBOARD). In Britain, wood was a universal building material, and since most of the country in earlier times was forested, mainly with hardwood trees, there was an abundant supply. Oak was the most popular type used for building due to its hard, weather-resistant properties. Since the logs were not used whole but split, this type of construction is sometimes described as *half-timbering*. The design of the timber frame varied but it was usually constructed on a low wall of stone, masonry or brick which was more resistant to wetness which might rise up from the ground. This supported a horizontal raft of timbers called a *plate* or *sill* which was attached to the base. Thick and strong upright posts, called *studs* were then fastened to the sill by mortising and their free upper ends were similarly attached to an-

other horizontal plate of timbers. This is known as the
WALL PLATE in a single storey timber-framed building and
it supports the RAFTERS of the roof. In buildings which are
two or even three storeys high, this upper plate is called
the BRESSUMER. In many timber-framed buildings, the upper storey is larger, and projects out over the lower one
and this is called a JETTY. The jetty is supported by a cross
BEAM running diagonally across the building which is
known as a *dragon beam*.

Timber-framed houses of the Elizabethan period and
later were often very decorative (*see* PARGETING). Any
wood infilling and BARGEBOARDS were ornately and intricately carved in a variety of different designs. Each storey was completed before an upper one was added and
many of the timbers were prepared in advance (*see* PRE-
FABRICATION) and the decorative pieces were carved in a
carpenter's workshop. Due to the durability of the oak
beams which were used, weather proofing applied to the
wood was in the form of light-coloured water-based
paint. The familiar black appearance of the wood in timber-framed buildings which we see today, was first applied during the 19th century and was a coal tar deriva-
tive.

timber truss a roof constructed from a framework of timbers (called the *truss*) which was open on the inside, i.e.
the beams could be viewed from the room below. the timber beams of the truss were securely fastened together
and so could support all the thrust and pressure exerted
by the roof. Timber truss construction evolved from the
earlier CRUCK type of roof and was in use by the early
Middle Ages. The design of the frame varied, generally

becoming more complicated as the centuries passed. In medieval times, the roof usually had a steeply pitched GABLE at either end and a long beam, called the *ridge piece*, stretched lengthways and horizontally beneath the apex. More roof beams, called *rafters*, extended from the WALL PLATE (*see* TIMBER FRAMING) to the ridge piece and these were angled so producing the pitch of the roof. Other horizontal beams known as PURLINS extended horizontally at right angles to the rafters. These were spaced at intervals down the pitch of the roof. Larger and more substantial rafters, called *principal rafters*, occurred at intervals, interspersed with the more slender *common rafters*. The principal rafters provided the support for the purlins. In many roofs, there was a substantial transverse timber, called a *tie-beam* extending across the width of the roof from side to side at the level of the wall plate. It was securely fastened to the wall plate at either side and often had a slight upward curvature at the centre. The tie beam counteracted the tendency for the weight of the roof to push the walls outwards. Running vertically from the centre of the tie beam to the roof apex, attached to the ridge piece at the top, were one or more wooden posts. A single one is known as a *king post*, but if two are present, these are called *queen posts*. Both provide additional support and help to strengthen the roof. Similar to a tie beam but at a higher level, further reinforcing timbers called *collar beams* were usually present and were fastened to the principal rafters on either side. Where the collar beam and principal rafters met, the angle was often infilled with a further wooden support which was curved at the base, called an *arched brace*. A similar reinforcement, but in the form of a straight strut, was alternatively fixed across the angle.

A variation on this design was the *coupled roof* which lacked collar beams or tie beams and gave a more lofty appearance inside. A more complicated form again, the *hammerbeam roof*, began to be built at the end of the 1300s. A series of truncated tie beams extending from the wall plate, called *hammer beams* were supported at their free ends by vertical *hammer posts* which joined a collar beam above. The angle between the two was reinforced with an arched brace and this type of roof was often richly carved and also painted, with the use of gilt. This was a design used in both church and domestic architecture.

torus a broad, convex moulding found, for example, around an attic BASE of a COLUMN, which has a semi-circular profile.

a decorated torus on a column base

tourelle a feature of French architecture but common in Scottish TOWER HOUSES, being a turret projecting out from the wall on CORBELS.

tower a tall structure which may be free-standing or part of a building and often with a circular plan, or it may be polygonal or square. Towers are a feature of many types of buildings, such as CASTLES, churches (to house the bells), great houses, public buildings (clock towers) or constructed singly as monuments or landmarks.

tower house a feature of medieval Scottish architecture built originally as fortified, defensive structures. They were tall with two or more storeys, the main hall being set above ground level. Versions were incorporated into later buildings although modified when there was less need to provide defence.

town house a house in a city, often built for a wealthy family and usually of a more modest size than a country mansion. Due to the high cost of building land in the cities, town houses have usually been narrow at the street front, extending backwards and upwards in order to gain space. By the late 1600s and 1700s, deceptively spacious town houses in the Classical style of the day were being built, often on three storeys with accommodation for servants at the top. In the 1800s, some town houses extended to four or five storeys and had a basement, the ground floor entrance on the street being reached by a flight of steps.

town planning the concept of town planning, i.e. the idea of viewing the layout of a town or city as a whole entity, has its origins in the ancient Classical world. In Greece during the 7th century BC, a plan based on a grid system, (known as *Milesian* after the coastal city of Miletus in Asia Minor) was developed. A Greek philosopher called Hippodamos developed the system further for the rebuilding of Miletus (after it had been destroyed by the

Persians) in 475 BC. The grid system consisted of a series of uniform streets crossing each other at right angles,
with building in the areas between them. In Miletus the
city was divided into three parts, one for temples and
worship, one for business, commerce and public buildings and one for private houses. As far as possible, the
Romans also used a grid system in the layout of their
towns and cities but modifications were made to take ac-
count of local geography and the need for defence. Considerable adaptations were sometimes required in the
towns which the Romans conquered and occupied in
more remote parts of the Empire.

Medieval European cities seldom developed to any particular plan, the prime aim being the need for defence.
Towns grew up around or near a CASTLE surrounded by
defensive walls. In Italy during the Renaissance period,
the architecture of ancient Rome, and the writings of
VITRUVIUS, were the main focus of interest. Several architects turned their thoughts to the design plan of a city as a
whole. There was renewed interest in the ideas of classical symmetry and the grid system, although usually these
plans were only carried out in the design and building of
some city centres. Renaissance ideas continued to influence town planning in all European countries, although
with national interpretations throughout the years that
followed. In the later 1800s in Britain and elsewhere in
Europe, there was a need to accommodate large numbers
of people, many of whom were forced to live in squalid
conditions. A number of architects became more interested in social concepts, and turned their thoughts away
from grand schemes in favour of providing decent hous-

ing, schools, hospitals and shops for working people. The few small towns that were built with these purposes in mind, such as Saltaire near Bradford, were the forerunners of the *Garden Cities* and *New Towns* which were built in the 20th century. During the 20th century, various schemes of town planning have been tried with differing degrees of success. After the Second World War in particular, there was an urgent need for rebuilding and for the provision of access for private and public transport. New Towns were built in Britain which, on the whole, have proved to be a success. In the present day, the need for careful town planning has never been more urgent and problems posed by road traffic versus population are very much to the fore.

trabeated post and lintel type construction as in the buildings of ancient Classical Greece, *see* CLASSICAL ARCHITECTURE.

tracery the intersecting ornamental stonework in the upper part of a Gothic window. Also, decorative work of a similar nature in arches, screens, vaults and panels which may be of stone or wood. Tracery developed during the early Gothic period when arched windows were divided into two panes or LIGHTS. The *dead* space above the lights at the top of the arch, known as the SPANDREL, had to be incorporated into the overall design. Hence this space was carved in curved shapes (known as FOIL), often with a simple quatrefoil design. This early tracery is called *plate tracery* and later designs developed from this type.

From the middle of the 1200s onwards, there was a narrowing of the stone infilling and the dividing bars and an increase in the area occupied by the glass. This type is known as *bar tracery* and a simple form is *Y tracery*. A single dividing bar branches into two at the top of the window arch in the shape of a curved letter Y. As time passed, tracery work became even more complicated with increasing numbers of bars and lights. Early patterns were formed from circles, called *geometrical tracery* but later OGEE shapes were used—*curvilinear* or *flowing tracery*. In *intersecting tracery* a series of mullions or bars cross one another at the top of the window arch, following the same line of curvature, to formed curved, diamond-shaped lights. *Reticulated tracery* is an elaboration of the curvilinear type, in which circles are drawn out into ogee shapes at the top and bottom. This form was popular in the first half of the 14th century. *Drop tracery* was another type which developed in the 14th and 15th centuries and was used to ornament an entrance arch. A tracery edging, often based on foils, projected into the space around the top of the arch. *Kentish tracery* which was mainly used in the county of Kent, was based on foils, but the bars were further elaborated into projecting knobs and barbs. *Flamboyant tracery* was derived from the curvilinear type and was a French form sometimes copied in England. Many ogee shapes were used to create an effect resembling tongues of flame. The last development in tracery work was during the 14th, 15th and 16th centuries and is *panel* or *rectilinear tracery*. Windows were divided by vertical and horizontal bars (MULLIONS and TRANSOMS) into panels. This reflected and complemented the wood panelling which was being used on walls and vaulted ceilings. Tracery work was less common and generally declined after the period of the Middle Ages.

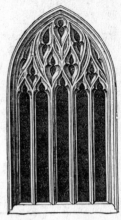

windows illustrating various styles of tracery

transept the side arms of a cross-shaped church which lie
in a north-south alignment.

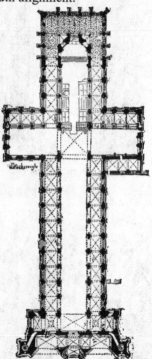

ground-plan of Peterborough Cathedral

transom horizontal dividing bar across a window or panel
which may be of wood, stone or metal.

transverse arch a type of arch which separates the bay of
one VAULT from an adjacent one, the division being

marked by a rib running transversely.

tribune has three meanings in architecture: 1) the APSE of a church built on the basilican plan or of a BASILICA; 2) a GALLERY in a church and 3) an elevated rostrum or platform.

trim a trimming which finishes the edge of a surface or opening. It is usually made of a different material, or varies in colour from the adjacent surface.

triumphal arch a feature of Roman architecture which was a free-standing commemorative arch dedicated to the Emperor or a military leader who had won a great victory.

triumphal arch of Constatntine at Rome

Some were constructed with three arches, a large central one and two similar smaller ones on either side. The large central one was for the passage of vehicles and the others for pedestrians as triumphal arches were usually built over a road. A CLASSICAL ORDER was used with COLUMNS and PILASTERS and the whole structure was richly and ornately carved and decorated. There was a dedicatory inscription above the cornice commemorating the person and/or event. Often there was a QUADRIGA on the top of the triumphal arch and it was a structure which was copied in later times, especially during the 18th and 19th centuries.

triglyph one of a number of blocks in a FRIEZE belonging to the DORIC ORDER (*see* CLASSICAL ORDER) with spaces in between called METOPES. The triglyphs are carved vertically with grooves called *glyphs*.

truss a number of timbers joined together to form a frame to carry other timbers, as in a TIMBER TRUSS roof.

decorated roof trusses

turret a small TOWER.

tympanum the space or face of a PEDIMENT in CLASSICAL ARCHITECTURE, which may be triangular or a segment of a circle and is edged by the sloping and horizontal mouldings of the CORNICE. Also, the space between a LINTEL of a doorway and an ARCH above.

U

undercroft a vaulted room or chamber which may be completely or partly underground, in a CASTLE, church or MANOR HOUSE which is for storage rather than a living area.

urban renewal the planning and restructuring of a city centre, town or village, usually involving widening and re-routing of roads to ease traffic congestion and improve living conditions.

V

vault an arched integral roof or ceiling originally constructed from stone, brick or masonry but later, in 18th and 19th century buildings, sometimes worked in wood or plaster.

vaults of the Cathedral at Spiers

Vaults were particularly characteristic of GOTHIC ARCHITEC-TURE during the Medieval period and also later during re-

217

vivals of this style. Roman builders used the simplest type of vault, the BARREL or tunnel vault but in the Middle Ages, vaulting became more complicated with the use of RIBS to develop elaborate patterns. The ribbed framework was constructed of stone and the area in between the ribs was infilled with stone, masonry or brick. It provided a strong structure and made it possible to construct high, divided vaults and to develop different designs. (*See* BARREL VAULT, CROWN, DOMICAL VAULT, FAN VAULT, PLOUGHSHARE VAULT, QUADRIPARTITE VAULT, RIDGE RIB, SEXPARTITE VAULT, SEVERY, STELLAR VAULT, TIERCERON, TRANSVERSE ARCH, VAULTING SHAFT).

vaulting shaft the upright, vertical shaft from which the main RIBS in a VAULT spring.

Venetian window this is also known as a *PALLADIAN* window or *serliana* and was derived from the work of PALLADIO. In this type of window there is a larger and taller central part which is arched, and this is flanked by two narrower lights on either side which have straight sides. A Venetian doorway follows the same pattern with the door occupying the central, larger arched space and with a narrower and lower oblong window on either side.

veranda (verandah) a type of BALCONY which is usually supported by metal supports, is roofed and may be glazed.

vestibule a usually small entrance hall or ANTEROOM.

viaduct an elevated road or railway carried on a series of arches.

villa in ancient Rome, a villa was a country MANSION HOUSE belonging to a well-to-do landowner. The term has continued to be applied to such a country residence in Italy, but in Britain it may refer to a more modest suburban house.

a Roman villa

Vitruvius Marcus Vitruvius Pollio lived during the first century BC and was a Roman architect and engineer. He wrote a ten volume work on architecture *De Architectura* which was dedicated to the Emperor Augustus. This had a tremendous impact on the work of later architects, especially during the Renaissance period, and so his influence continued for many hundreds of years after his death.

volute a spiral SCROLL like a coiled shell which is typical of a CAPITAL of the Ionic order (see CLASSICAL ORDER). Smaller volutes may also be found on corinthian and composite capitals.

voussoirs the wedge-shaped blocks of stone which form the curve of an ARCH.

vyse a spiral STAIRCASE.

W

wainscot timber lining or panelling on walls. Originally it referred to rough oak planks and it was used extensively in Elizabethan building.

wall-plate in roofing, a timber that is laid along the top of the wall to which the ends of the rafters are fastened. Also, in a timber-framed building elements of the wall below (e.g. the studs) are fastened to the wall plate by tenoned joints.

ward *see* **bailey**

wattle and daub a method of wall construction used to fill between the members of timber-framed houses. It comprises branches or thin laths (the wattles) upon which is plastered clay or mud (the daub).

weatherboard a method of cladding in which boards are attached to exterior walls. The boards are fixed vertically or horizontally, and often overlap although they can be tongued and grooved. If fitted horizontally, the upper edge of the board is usually thinner than the lower edge. Weatherboarding was common in Scandinavia and northern Europe. In North America it is called clapboarding.

weathering the sloping surface of a sill, parapet, buttress, or similar feature which throws off rainwater. Also the degradation of building materials due to action of the weather. In addition to rain, frost and wind, other agents include pollution, ultraviolet light and salt air. With time, architectural features in stone can be blurred and details lost.

Modern materials are equally prone to weathering and

concrete is no exception, although it will depend upon the quality of the concrete. Acid attack from a polluted atmosphere is common but it may also suffer deposition of dirt, colonization by algae or lichen and deposition of salts from the concrete as the surface layers react with gases in the air. Buildings can be designed to control weathering by judicious use of materials and design features, including in particular the need to avoid concentrations of water.

web in a vault, the cell or bay between ribs.

window an opening in a wall for purposes of lighting or ventilation, which also permits those inside to view the surroundings. In early constructions (early Medieval) the windows were basically slits in the walls. The knowledge of buildings was such at that time that it was thought inadvisable to have large openings which might weaken the walls. Also, smaller openings were more easily defended and in the absence of glass, windows were covered by wooden shutters which, in addition to blocking out the weather, also cut out the light.

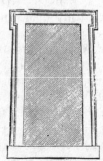

typical shape of Grecian window

Saxon windows also tended to be small with round or triangular heads, the latter created by long stones leaning against each other and on the imposts. Often, and especially in churches, the windows are formed of two lights or more, separated by pillars. Glazed Saxon windows also commonly exhibit internal SPLAYS. Early Norman windows are similar in many respects with semi-circular heads, internal splays and initially small sizes which in time increased. Ornament was kept to a minimum although some exhibit mouldings in the arch or jambs.

Long narrow windows in groups or placed singly with arched heads characterizes the Early English style. Internal splays and detached supporting pillars within the window opening are also found. The degree of decoration varies enormously and circular windows are not uncommon. In the 14th century the windows were larger, divided into lights by mullions and with heads of various styles, although the commonest is the pointed arch. Tracery became a feature as did ball-flower moulding in windows of the Decorated period. Moving into the Perpendicular period, the window shape was essentially the same but with different tracery and heads and altered mouldings.

Window areas increased in the 16th century with small panes held by lead bars (*cames*). Also it became possible to open parts of windows and eventually a large part of a CASEMENT window was made to open. Renaissance windows adopted a classical style with rectangular panes and the sash window came to prominence. The Regency period was known for its bow-fronted windows and in due course advances in glass technology enabled the production of large windows with just two panes.

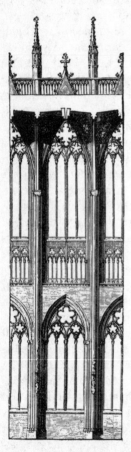
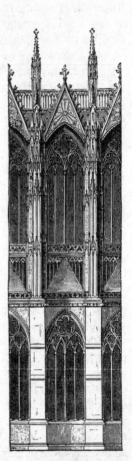

internal and external view of windows at Cologne Cathedral

The 20th century has seen tremendous developments in GLASS technology and its subsequent incorporation in windows. Use of metal frames, latterly aluminium, and uPVC and recently double glazing has enabled windows to fulfil an aesthetic as well as utilitarian function. (*See individual entries for further details*).

ARCHITECTS

Aalto, Hugo A.V. (Finnish) b.1898
Notable works: Finlandia Concert Hall, Helsinki; Massachusetts Institute of Technology student hostel

Abramovitz, Max (American) b.1908
Notable works: Krannert Centre, University of Illionois

Adam, Robert (Scottish) b.1728
Notable works: Culzean Castle, Ayrshire; Harewood House near Leeds; Keddleston House in Derbyshire

Aillaud, Émile (French) b.1902
Notable works: Les Courtillières housing estate, near Paris

Alberti, Leone B (Italian) b.1404
Notable works: Palazzo Rucellai, Florence; churches at Mantua

Albini, Franco (Italian) b.1905
Notable works: Municipal office, Genoa

Aldrich, Henry (English) b.1648
Notable works: All Saints', Oxford

Aleijadinho, Antonio F.L. (Brazilian) b.1738
Notable works: São Francisco, Ouro Preto

Alessi, Galeazzo (Italian) b.1512
Notable works: Palazzo Marino

Alexander, Christopher (English) b.1936
Notable works: Mexican housing at Mexicali

Alfieri, Benedetto (Italian) b.1699
Notable works: Carignano Parish Church

Algardi, Alessandro (Italian) b.1595
Notable works: Villa Doria-Pamphili, Rome

Almquist, Osvald (Swedish) b.1884
Notable works: hydro-electric power plants

Amadeo, Giovanni A. (Italian) b.1447
Notable works: façade of the Cortosa outside Pavia

Ammanati, Bartolomeo (Italian) b.1511
Notable works: Tempietto della Vittoria near Arezzo

Ando, Tadao (Japanese) b.1941
Notable works: domestic house design

Andrews, John (Australian) b.1933
Notable works: Canadian National Tower, Toronto

Antoine, Jacques-Denis (French) b.1733
Notable works: the Mint, Paris

Antonelli, Alessandro (Italian) b.1798
Notable works: Novara Cathedral

Archer, Thomas (English) b.1668
Notable works: St John Church, Smith Square, London

Asplund, Gunnar E. (Swedish) b.1885
Notable works: extension to Göteborg Town Hall

Aymonino, Carlo (Italian) b.1926
Notable works: city centre design; Turin, Florence

Bähr, Georg (German) b.1666
Notable works: Frauenkirche, Dresden (destroyed in World War II)

Baker, Sir Herbert (English) b.1862
Notable works: Bank of England and Church House, Westminster; government buildings in Pretoria

Baltard, Victor (French) b.1805
Notable works: Les Halles, Paris

Barragán, Luis (Mexican) b.1902
Notable works: Mexico city suburbs

Barry, Sir Charles (English) b.1795
Notable works: Houses of Parliament

Bawa, Geoffrey (Sri Lankan) b.1919
Notable works: University of Ruhuna, Matara

Bazhenov, Vasily (Russian) b.1738
Notable works: Yushkov House, Moscow

Beer, Michael (German) d.1666
Notable works: Benedictine Abbey Church, Weingarten

Behrens, Peter (German) b.1868
Notable works: A.E.G. turbine factory, Berlin

Bélanger, François-Joseph (French) 1744
Notable works: Bagatelle, Bois de Boulogne, Paris

Bentley, John F. (English) 1839
Notable works: Westminster Cathedral, London

Berlage, Hendrik P. (Dutch)1856
Notable works: Amsterdam Exchange

Bernini, Giovanni Lorenzo (Italian) b.1598
Notable works: Palazzo Odescalchi, the colonnade at St
Peters, Rome

Bertotti-Scamozzi, Ottavio (Italian) b.1719
Notable works: Palazzo Franceschini, Vicenza

Bodley, George F. (Scottish) b.1827
Notable works: Queen's College Chapel, Cambridge

Boffrand, Gabriel G. (French) b.1667
Notable works: Château de Saint Ouen

Bofill, Ricardo (Spanish) b.1939
Notable works: housing complexes

Böhm, Dominikus (German) b.1880
Notable works: St Engelbert Church, Cologne- Riehl

Böhm, Gottfried (German) b.1920
Notable works: Town Hall, Bensberg

Boileau, Louis-Auguste (French) b.1812
Notable works: St Eugène, Paris

Bonatz, Paul (German) b.1877
Notable works: Stuttgart railway station

Bonomi, Joseph (Italian) b.1739
Notable works: St James Church, Great Packington,
Warwickshire

Borromini, Francesco (Italian) b.1599
Notable works: S. Carlo alle Quattro Fontane

Botta, Mario (Swiss) b.1943
Notable works: Casa Rotondo, Stabio

Boullée, Étienne-Louis (French) b.1728
Notable works: Hôtel Alexandre, Paris

Bramante, Donato (Italian) d. 1514
St Peter's Basilica, Rome; parts of the Vatican palace;
Church of Santa Maria delle Grazie, Milan

Brever, Marcel (Hungarian) b.1902
Notable works: Whitney Museum, New York

Brodrick, Cuthbert (English) b.1822
Notable works: Hull and Leeds Town Halls

Brooks, James (English) b.1825
Notable works: Holy Saviour Church, Hoxton

Brown, Lancelot ('Capability' Brown) (English) b.1716
Notable works: Claremount House, the gardens of
Harewood and Blenheim Houses

Bruce, Sir William (Scottish) b.1630
Notable works: Hopetoun House

Brunelleschi, Filippo (Italian) b.1377
Notable works: dome of Florence Cathedral

Bulfinch, Charles (American) b.1763
Notable works: Boston State House

Burges, William (English) b.1827
Notable works: Cork Cathedral

Burlington, Richard B. (English) b.1694
Notable works: Assembly Rooms, York

...iam, Daniel H. (American) b.1846
...le works: Monadnock building, Chicago

...on, Decimus (English) b.1800
...ible works: Colosseum, Regent's Park

...terfield, William (English) b.1814
...otable works: All Saints Church, London; Keble College, Oxford

Cagnola, Marchese L. (Italian) b.1762
Notable works: Arco della Pace, Milan

Cameron, Charles (English) b.1743
Notable works: great palace at Pavlovsk, Russia

Campen, Jacob van (Dutch) b.1595
Notable works: Town Hall (Royal Palace), Amsterdam

Candela, Felix (Spanish) b.1910
Notable works: Church of Our Lady of Miracles, Mexico City.

Carr, John (English) b.1723
Notable works: The Crescent, Buxton

Castle, Richard (German) b.1690
Notable works: Leinster House, Dublin

Chalgrin, Jean (French) b.1739
Notable works: Arc de Triomphe, Paris

...ambers, Sir William (Swedish) b.1723
...able works: Somerset House, London

...vakinsky, Savva (Russian) b.1713
...ble works: St Nicholas Cathedral, Leningrad

Chiaveri, Gaetano (Italian) b.1689
Notable works: Hofkirche, Dresden

Churriguera, José de (Spanish) b.1665
Notable works: ornamentation style

Coates, Wells (English) b.1895
Notable works: Palace Gate flats, London

Cockerell, Charles R. (English) b.1788
Notable works: Cambridge University Library

Cockerell, Samuel P. (English) b.1753
Notable works: Sezincote House

Codussi, Mauro (Italian) b.1440
Notable works: numerous palaces

Comper, John N. (English) b.1864
Notable works: St Mary's Church, Wellingborough

Corrca, Charles M. (Indian) b.1930
Notable works: Parliament Buildings, Bhopal

Costa, Lucio (Brazilian) b.1902
Notable works: designer of plans for Brasilia, Brazil

Covarrubias, Alonso de (Spanish) b.1488
Notable works: Chapel of the New Kings, Toledo Cathedral

Cram, Ralph A. (American) b.1863
Notable works: Cathedral of St John the Divine, New York

Cubitt, Thomas (English) b.1788
Notable works: Gordon and Eaton Squares, London

Cuvilliés, François (French) b.1695
Notable works: Residenztheater, München

Cuypers, Petrus J.H. (Dutch) b.1827
Notable works: Central Station, Amsterdam

Dance, George (English) b.1741
Notable works: Mansion House, London

Davis, Alexander J. (American) b.1903
Notable works: United States Custom House, New York

Dientzenhofer, Georg (German) b.1643
Notable works: Church at Kappel

Dientzenhofer, Johann (German) b.1663
Notable works: Abbey at Banz

Dientzenhofer, Kilian I. (German) b.1689
Notable works: Thomas Kirche, Prague

Dobson, John (English) b.1787
Notable works: Central Railway Station, Newcastle

Du Ry, Paul (French) b.1640
Notable works: various buildings in Kassel

Dudok, Willem M. (Dutch) b.1884
Notable works: Hilversum Town Hall

Effner, Joseph (German) b.1687
Notable works: Gallery of Ancestors, Münich

Eiffel, Gustave (French) b.1832
Notable works: Eiffel Tower, Paris

Eigtued, Nils (Danish) b.1701
Notable works: Amalienborg, Copenhagen

Ellis, Peter (English) b.1804
Notable works: Oriel Chambers, Liverpool

Engel, Carl L. (German) b.1778
Notable works: Helsinki Cathedral

Erdmannsdorf, Friedrich W. (German) b.1736
Notable works: Wörlitz palace

Erickson, Arthur C. (Canadian) b.1924
Notable works: Government offices, Vancouver

Erskine, Ralph (English) b.1914
Notable works: Byker housing, Newcastle

Fathy, Hassan (Egyptian) b.1900
Notable works: village of New Gournia, Luxor

Figini, Luigi (Italian) b.1903
Notable works: Olivetti H.Q., Iurea

Figueroa, Leonardo de (Spanish) b.1650
Notable works: Salvador Church, Seville

Fischer, Johann M. (German) b.1692
Notable works: Benedictine Abbey Church, Ottobeuren

Fischer von Erlach, Johann B. (Austrian) b.1656
Notable works: Karlskirche, Vienna

Flitcroft, Henry (English) b.1697
Notable works: Chatham House; Woburn Abbey

Floris, Cornelis (Dutch) b.1514
Notable works: Antwerp Town Hall

Fontaine, Pierre (French) b.1762
Notable works: Palais Royal restoration, Paris

Fontana, Carlo (Italian) b.1638
Notable works: St Peter's baptismal chapel, Rome

Fontana, Domenico (Italian) b.1543
Notable works: Vatican Library

Foster, Norman (English) b.1935
Notable works: HQ of the Hong Kong bank

Freyssinet, Eugène (French) b.1879
Notable works: St Michael Bridge, Toulouse

Fry, Edwin M. (English) b.1899
Notable works: Impington Village College

Fuga, Ferdinando (Italian) b.1699
Notable works: Palazzo Corsini, Rome

Fuller, Richard B. (American) b.1895
Notable works: US pavilion, Montreal Exhibition

Furness, Frank (American) b.1839
Notable works: Pennsylvania Academy of Fine Arts

Gabriel, Ange-Jacques (French) b.1698
Notable works: Petit Trianon, Versailles

Galilei, Alessandro M.G. (Italian) b.1691
Notable works: Corsini Chapel, Rome

Gandon, James (Irish) b.1743
Notable works: Four Courts, Dublin

Gärtner, Friedrich von (German) b.1792
Notable works: State Library, München

Gaudi y Cornet, Antonio (Spanish) b.1852
Notable works: Casa Vicens, Barcelona

Gibberd, Sir Frederick (English) b.1908
Notable works: buildings in Harlow New Town

Gibbs, James (Scottish) b.1662
Notable works: St Martin-in-the-Fields, London

Gilbert, Cass (American) b.1859
Notable works: Woolworth Building, New York

Gill, Irving John (American) b.1870
Notable works: Laughlin House, Los Angeles

Godefroy, Maximilien (French) b.1765
Notable works: Battle Monument, Baltimore

Godwin, Edward M. (English) b.1833
Notable works: Congleton Town Hall

Goff, Bruce A. (American) b.1904
Notable works: Ford House, Aurora, Illinois

Gondovin, Jacques (French) b.1737
Notable works: École de Chirurgie, Paris

Goodhue, Bertram G. (American) b.1869
Notable works: Nebraska State Capitol, Lincoln

Graves, Michael (American) b.1934
Notable works: Public Services Building, Portland,
Oregon

Greenway, Francis H. (English) b.1777
Notable works: Assembly Rooms, Bristol

Griffin, Walter B. (American) b.1876
Notable works: Capitol Theatre, Melbourne

Gropius, Walter (German) b.1883
Notable works: Bauhaus building, Dessau; Pan Am
Building, New York; US Embassy, Athens

Hadfield, George (English) b.1763
Notable works: City Hall, Washington

Hamilton, Thomas (Scottish) b.1784
Notable works: Royal High School, Edinburgh

Hansen, Theophil von (Danish) b.1813
Notable works: Stock Exchange, Vienna

Hardovin-Mansart, Jules (French) b.1646
Notable works: extensions to Versailles

Hardwick, Philip (English) b.1792
Notable works: Euston Station, London

Harrison, Peter (American) b.1716
Notable works: Christ Church, Cambridge, Massachusetts

Harrison, Thomas (English) b.1744
Notable works: Chester Castle

Harrison, Wallace K. (American) b.1895
Notable works: Rockefeller Center, New York

Haviland, John (American) b.1792
Notable works: Eastern Penitentiary, Philadelphia

Hawksmoor, Nicholas (English) b.1661
Notable works: St George's Church, Bloomsbury

Hennebique, François (French) b.1842
Notable works: numerous concrete structures

Hentrich, Helmut (German) b.1905
Notable works: University buildings, Bochum

Hildebrandt, Johann L. von (Austrian) b.1668
Notable works: Schloss Mirabell, Salzburg

Hittorf, Jakob I. (German) b.1792
Notable works: St Vincent de Paul, Paris

Hoban, James (Irish) b.1762
Notable works: White House, Washington

Holden, Charles (English) b.1876
Notable works: Bristol Public Library

Holl, Elias (German) b.1573
Notable works: Town Hall, Augsburg

Holland, Henry (English) b.1745
Notable works: Carlton House, London

Hollein, Hans (Austrian) b.1934
Notable works: Abteilberg Museum, Mönchengladbach

Hood, Raymond M. (American) b.1881
Notable works: McGraw-Hill Building, New York

Hopkins, Michael (English) b.1935
Notable works: Schlumberger Laboratories, Cambridge

Horta, Baron V. (Belgian) b.1861
Notable works:Hôtel Tassel, Brussels

Hunt, Richard M. (American) b.1827
Notable works: Tribune building, New York

Inwood, Henry W. (English) b.1794
Notable works: St Pancras Church, London

Isozaki, Arata (Japanese) b.1931
Notable works: Civic Centre, Tsukuba

Jacobsen, Arne (Swedish) b.1902
Notable works: Town Hall, Aarhus

James, John (English) b.1672
Notable works: St George's, Hanover Square, London

Japelli, Giuseppe (Italian) b.1783
Notable works: Teatro Verdi, Padua

Jefferson, Thomas (American) b.1743
Notable works: Virginia State Capitol

Johnson, Philip C. (American) b.1906
Notable works: New York State Theater; IDS Centre, Minneapolis; Pennziol Place, Houston

Jones, Inigo (English) b.1573
Notable works: Banqueting House; Queen's House; layout for Covent Garden, London

Jourdain, Frantz (French) b.1847
Notable works: La Samaritaine department store, Paris

Jussow, Heinrich C. (German) b.1754
Notable works: Löwenburg castle

Juvarro, Filippo (Italian) b.1678
Notable works: the chapel of the Venaria Reale, Turin

Kahn, Albert (German) b.1869
Notable works: Ford Motor Co. factories

Kahn, Louis I. (Estonian) b.1901
Notable works: Yale University Art Gallery

Kazakov, Matyey F. (Russian) b.1738
Notable works: Kremlin Senate building

Kent, William (English) b.1685
Notable works: the Treasury, London; Holkham Hall

Key, Lieven de (Dutch) b.1560
Notable works: Leiden Town Hall façade

Kikutake, K. (Japanese) b.1928
Notable works: Miyakonoyo Town Hall

Klenze, Leo von (German) b.1784
Notable works: Propylaea, München

Klint, Peder V.J. (Danish) b.1853
Notable works: Grundtuig church, Copenhagen

Langhans, Carl G. (German) b.1732
Notable works: Brandenburg Gate, Berlin

Latrobe, Benjamin H. (Moravian) b.1764
Notable works: Bank of Pennsylvania

Laves, Georg L.F. (German) b.1788
Notable works: Wagenheim Palace

Le Corbusier, Charles (French) b.1887
Notable works: Unité de'Habitation, Marseiles; Swiss House, Paris; Ronchamp Church; Museum of Modern Art, Tokyo

Le Vau, Louis (French) b.1612
Notable works: Collège des Quatres Nations, Paris

Ledoux, Claude N. (French) b.1736
Notable works: Château de Bénouville, Paris

L'Enfant, Pierre C. (French) b.1754
Notable works: old City Hall, New York

Leoni, Giacomo (Italian) b.1686
Notable works: Queensbury House, London

Lethaby, William R. (English) b.1857
Notable works: Brockhampton Church, Herefordshire

Longhena, Baldassare (Italian) b.1597
Notable works: numerous palaces

Loos, Adolf (Austrian) b.1870
Notable works: municipal housing in Vienna

Louis, Victor (French) b.1731
Notable works: Bordeaux theatre

Lutyens, Sir Edwin (English) b.1869
Notable works: Cenotaph in Whitehall, London; British Embassy, Washington; Gladstone Hall, Yorkshire

Mackintosh, Charles R. (Scottish) b.1868
Notable works: Glasgow School of Art; Hill House, Helensborough

Maillart, Robert (Swiss) b.1872
Notable works: Tavenasa Bridge

Mansart, François (French) b.1598
Notable works: Maisons Lafitte, Paris

Mansart, Jules Hardouin (French) b.1646
Notable works: Dôme des Invalides, Paris

Markelius, Sven G. (Swedish) b.1889
Notable works: Vällingby (suburb of Stockholm)

Martin, Sir Leslie (English) b.1908
Notable works: Roehampton housing estate

Massari, Giorgio (Italian) b.1687
Notable works: Palazzo Grassi, Venice

Matthew, Sir Robert Hogg (English) b.1906
Notable works: York University

May, Hugh (English) b.1621
Notable works: Eltham Lodge, London

Mayekawa, Kunio (Japanese) b.1905
Notable works: Tokyo Metropolitan Festival Hall

McIntire, Samuel (American) b.1757
Notable works: Salem Court House (now demolished)

McKim, Charles F. (American) b.1847
Notable works: Columbia University, New York

Mendelsohn, Erich (German) b.1887
Notable works: Potsdam Obsrevatory; Columbushaus,Berlin

Michelangelo, Buonarroti (Italian) b.1475
Notable works: reconstructed the Capitol in Rome;
completion of St Peter's, Rome

Michelozzo, Bartolommeo di (Italian) b.1396
Notable works: Portinari chapel, Milan

Mies van der Rohe, Ludwig (German) b.1886
Notable works: Pavilion at the 1929 Barcelona Exhibition; IBM building, Chicago; Seagram Building, New York

Mills, Robert (American) b.1781
Notable works: Washington Monument, Washington

Moore, Charles W. (American) b.1925
Notable works: Kresge College, UC Santa Cruz

Morandi, Riccardo (Italian) b.1902
Notable works: Maracaibo bridge, Venezuela

Morris, Roger (English) b.1695
Notable works: White Lodge, Richmond

Mosbrugger, Caspar (Swiss) b.1656
Notable works: Einsiedeln abbey church

Mylne, Robert (Scottish) b.1733
Notable works: Blackfriars Bridge, London

Nash, John (English) b.1752
Notable works: developed London's West End; Brighton Pavilion

Nervi, Pier Luigi (Italian) b.1891
Notable works: Pirelli skyscraper, Milan

Neumann, Johann B. (German) b.1687 *Notable works*: pilgrimage church of Vierzehn heiligen

Neutra, Richard J. (Austrian) b.1892
Notable works: Lovell Health House, Los Angeles

Niemeyer, Oscar (Brazilian) b.1907
Notable works: church of St Francis at Pampulha; many public buildings in Brasilia

Olbrich, Joseph M. (Austrian) b.1867
Notable works: Tietz department store, Düsseldorf

Østberg, Ragnar (Swedish) b.1866
Notable works: Stockholm City Hall

Otto, Frei (German) b.1925
Notable works: German Pavilion, Montreal

Paine, James (English) b.1717
Notable works: Wardour Castle

Palladio, Andrea (Italian) b.1508
Notable works: Teatro Olimpico, Vicenza; churches of S. Giorgio Maggiore and Il Redentore, Venice

Papworth, John B. (English) b.1775
Notable works: Lansdown Crescent, Cheltenham

Paxton, Sir Joseph (English) b.1803
Notable works: Crystal Palace

Pearce, Sir Edward L. (Irish) b.1699
Notable works: Parliament House, Dublin

Pearson, John L. (English) b.1817
Notable works: Truro Cathedral

Pei, Ieoh M. (American) b.1917
Notable works: John F. Kennedy Library, the John Hancock Tower, Boston; Place Ville-Marie, Montreal

Peruzzi, Baldassare (Italian) b.1481
Notable works: Palazzo Massimo alle Colonne, Rome

Piano, Renzo (Italian) b.1937
Notable works: Pompidou Centre, Paris

Playfair, William H. (Scottish) b.1790
Notable works: Royal Scottish Academy

Pollak, Leopoldo (Austrian) b.1751
Notable works: Villa Belgioioso Reale

Pollak, Mihály (Hungarian) b.1773
Notable works: Theatre and Assembly Rooms, Budapest

Ponti, Gio (Italian) b.1891
Notable works: Pirelli skyscraper, Milan (with Nervi)

Pöppelman, Matthaus D. (German) b.1662
Notable works: the Zwinger, Dresden

Post, George B. (American) b.1837
Notable works: New York Times building

Post, Pieter (Dutch) b.1608
Notable works: Town Hall, Maastricht

Prandtauer, Jakob (Austrian) b.1660
Notable works: Melk abbey

Pratt, Sir Roger (English) b.1620
Notable works: Clarendon House, London (now destroyed)

Prouvé, Jean (French) b.1901
Notable works: Spa building, Evian

Pugin, Augustus W.N. (English) b.1812
Notable works: Nottingham Cathedral; Birmingham Cathedral

Quarenghi, Giacomo (Italian) b.1744
Notable works: Academy of Sciences, Leningrad

Raphael (Raffaello), Sanzio (Italian) b.1483
Notable works: Palazzo Pandolfini, Florence

Rennie, John (Scottish) b.1761
Notable works: Southwark, Waterloo and London Bridges; Plymouth breakwater

Renwick, James (English) b.1818
Notable works: Smithsonian Institute, Washington

Ribera, Pedro de (Spanish) b.1683
Notable works: Toledo bridge

Richardson, Henry H. (American) b.1838
Notable works: Austin Hall, Harvard

Rickman, Thomas (English) b.1776
Notable works: New Court, St John's Cambridge

Roche, Eamonn K. (Irish) b.1922
Notable works: United Nation Plaza Hotel, New York

Rodriguez Tizon, Ventura (Spanish) b.1717
Notable works: Pamplona Cathedral

Rogers, Isaiah (American) b.1800
Notable works: Bank of America, New York

Rogers, Richard (English) b.1933
Notable works: Lloyd's of London building

Rossi, Giovanni A. de' (Italian) b.1616
Notable works: Palazzo Altieri, Rome

Rossi, Karl I. (Russian) b.1775
Notable works: New Michael Palace, Leningrad

Saarinen, Eero (Finnish) b.1910
Notable works: US Embassy, London

Saarinen, Eliel (Finnish) b.1873
Notable works: Railway Station, Helsinki

Safdie, Moshe (Israeli) b.1938
Notable works: Yeshivat Porat Yosef Rabbinical College

Salvin, Anthony (English) b.1799
Notable works: Peckforton Castle, Cheshire

Sangallo, Antonio da (Italian) b.1483
Notable works: Palazzo Farnese, Rome

Sangallo, Giuliano da (Italian) b.1445
Notable works: Palazzo Gondi, Florence

Sanmicheli, Michele (Italian) b.1484
Notable works: Porta Palio, Verona

Scamozzi, Vincenzo (Italian) b.1552
Notable works: Villa Rocca Pisana, Lonigo

Scharoun, Hans (German) b.1893
Notable works: German Embassy, Brasilia

Schickhardt, Heinrich (German) b.1558
Notable works: wing of the Schloss, Stuttgart (now destroyed)

Schindler, Rudolph M. (German) b.1887
Notable works: Beach House, Newport beach

Schinkel, Karl F. (German) b.1781
Notable works: Old Museum, Berlin

Scott, Sir George Gilbert (English) b.1811
Notable works: St Pancreas Hotel, London; St Nicholas's Church, Hamburg

Scott, Sir Giles Gilbert (English) b.1880
Notable works: Liverpool Cathedral; Waterloo Bridge

Seddon, John P. (English) b.1827
Notable works: hotel (now University), Aberystwyth

Semper, Gottfried (German) b.1803
Notable works: the Opera, Dresden

Sheppard, Richard (English) b.1910
Notable works: Churchilll College, Cambridge

Sinan (Turkish) b.1489
Notable works: mosques at Edirne and Istanbul

Smirke, Sir Robert (English) b.1780
Notable works: British Museum, London

Soane, Sir John (English) b.1753
Notable works: Bank of England; St Peter's, Walworth

Solari, Santino (Italian) b.1576
Notable works: Salzburg Cathedral

Soleri, Paolo (Italian) b.1919
Notable works: Solimene ceramics factory, Salerno

Sommaruga, Giuseppe (Italian) b.1867
Notable works: Palazzo Castiglioni, Milan

Soufflot, Jacques G. (French) b.1713
Notable works: Hotel Dieu, Lyon

Starov, Ivan Y. (Russian) b.1744
Notable works: Tauride Palace, Petersburg

Stasov, Vasily P. (Russian) b.1769
Notable works: Moscow Gate

Stirling, James (English) b.1926
Notable works: Neuestaatsgalerie, Stuttgart

Stone, Edward D. (American) b.1902
Notable works: US Embassy, New Delhi

Street, George E. (English) b.1824
Notable works: All Saints Church, Clifton, Bristol

Strickland, William (American) b.1788
Notable works: Tennessee State Capitol, Nashville

Stuart, James (English) b.1713
Notable works: temple, Hagley

Talman, William (English) b.1650
Notable works: Chatsworth House, south and east front

Tange, Kenzo (Japanese) b.1913
Notable works: Akasaka Prince Hotel, Tokyo

Telford, Thomas (Scottish) b.1757
Notable works: Dean Bridge, Edinburgh; Caledonian Canal

Tessin, Nicodemus (Swedish) b.1615
Notable works: Göteborg Town Hall

Thomson, Alexander (Scottish) b.1817
Notable works: St Vincent Street Church, Glasgow

Torroja, Eduardo (Spanish) b.1899
Notable works: Algeciras Market Hall

Townsend, Charles H. (English) b.1851
Notable works: Horniman Museum, London

Trezzini, Domenico (Swiss) b.1670
Notable works: Cathedral of St Peter and Paul, St Petersburg

Upjohn, Richard (English) b.1802
Notable works: Trinity Church, New York

Vaccarini, Giovan B. (Italian) b.1702
Notable works: Catania cathedral

Vanbrugh, Sir John (English) b.1664
Notable works: Castle Howard, near Leeds

Vanvitelli, Luigi (Italian) b.1700
Notable works: palace at Caserta, Naples

Vardy, John (English) b.1718
Notable works: Spencer House, London

Velde, Henry van de (Belgian) b.1863
Notable works: University library, Ghent

Venturi, Robert (American) b.1925
Notable works: extension to National Gallery, London

Vicente de Oliveira, Mateus (Portuguese) b.1710
Notable works: palace of Queluz

Vignola, Giacomo B. (Italian) b.1507
Notable works: Villa Giulia, Rome

Vignon, Pierre A. (French) b.1762
Notable works: the Madeleine, Paris

Villanueva, Juan de (Spanish) b.1739
Notable works: Prado Museum, Madrid

Waterhouse, Alfred (English) b.1830
Notable works: Natural History Museum, Prudential Building, St Paul's School, London

Webb, Sir Aston (English) b.1849
Notable works: East front of Buckingham Palace, Victoria and Albert Museum, London

Wilkins, William (English) b.1778
Notable works: Downing College, Cambridge

Wood, John (elder) (English) b.1704
Notable works: Queen Square and others, Bath

Wood, John (younger) (English) b.1728
Notable works: Royal Crescent, Bath

Wren, Sir Christopher (English) b.1632
Notable works: St Paul's Cathedral; Royal Hospital, Chelsea; Kensington Palace; Trinity College Library, Cambridge

Wright, Frank Lloyd (American) b.1869
Notable works: Larkin Building, Buffalo; Imperial Hotel, Tokyo; Guggenheim Museum, New York

Wyatt, Benjamin D. (English) b.1775
Notable works: Drury Lane Theatre, London

Wyatt, James (English) b.1746
Notable works: Castle Coole, N. Ireland

Wyatt, Samuel (English) b.1737
Notable works: Doddington Hall, Cheshire

Yamasaki, Minoru (American) b.1912
Notable works: American Concrete Institute, Detroit

Zakharov, Andreyan D. (Russian) b.1761
Notable works: the Admiralty, Leningrad

Zimmermann, Dominikus (German) b.1685
Notable works: Frauenkirche, Günzburg